happy starts AT home

happy starts AT home

CHANGE YOUR SPACE, TRANSFORM YOUR LIFE

REBECCA WEST

CICO BOOKS
LONDON NEW YORK

Published in 2020 by CICO Books
An imprint of Ryland Peters & Small Ltd
20–21 Jockey's Fields   341 E 116th St
London WC1R 4BW   New York, NY 10029

www.rylandpeters.com

10 9 8 7 6 5 4 3 2 1

A CIP catalog record for this book is available from
the Library of Congress and the British Library.

ISBN: 978-1-78249-845-2

Printed in China

Designer: Geoff Borin
Photographer: for all photography credits, see page 175

Commissioning editor: Kristine Pidkameny
In-house editor: Anna Galkina
Art director: Sally Powell
Head of production: Patricia Harrington
Publishing manager: Penny Craig
Publisher: Cindy Richards

CONTENTS

introduction

It's not about buying or not buying a new sofa. It's about whether your home is working for you.

Your home can be the key to better health, better sleep, better relationships, and an all-round better life. Your home can also lock you into a damaging relationship, drain your energy, and devour your money. Every choice you make about your home influences your life. With every dollar you spend on your home, you cast a vote for the kind of life you wish to live: what you value, how you will be treated, and whom you will let in. It's that powerful! If you're like me, you are highly affected by your environment. In a messy room we feel frustrated, stressed, even out of control.

We crave the beauty and calm depicted in glossy home decorating magazines—not just because the pictures are pretty, but because we imagine that if we could just get our homes close to that ideal, we'd enjoy less stressful, more contented lives. The truth is your home can directly improve your well-being and contentment. It can help decrease your stress level and increase your happiness. But not necessarily by looking like the cover of an interior design magazine. This book is about using your home as a tool to make change happen in your life.

Being happy at home isn't about having a Pinterest-perfect space or expensive furnishings. It's about having a home that works for you, supports your dreams, and helps you feel secure.

getting started

I became a designer by chance, not by, well, design. Nearly a decade ago I found myself divorced and living in a house that constantly reminded me of my failed marriage. I got tired of living somewhere that reverberated with sadness, loss, and defeat. After about six months of feeling stuck, I repainted the walls and completely refurnished the house (and it didn't take buckets of money). Here's what I discovered: Changing what I saw around me transformed how I saw my future. And that change thrilled me. While I hadn't moved physically, I had moved on psychologically.

I started my design company, Seriously Happy Homes, because I am passionate about helping people experience the transformative power of the home. I feel a special connection to those who are in life transition or who may feel blocked, frustrated, or trapped, like I once did. So, while I did go back to school to earn a degree in interior design, I didn't start my company out of a love for design per se. I started it to help people use their home as a tool for change. To this day I don't really care whether you buy a new sofa. I do care that your home is working for you. I want to share with you the tools you need to create your own happy home. It's not about copying design trends. It's about figuring out what you need from your home, and then identifying how to make your home work for you.

first, let's ask why

A lot of books out there tell you how to declutter, decorate, and design your home, but many skip the most important question—why? Why have you decided to change something about your home? Why spend your time, money, and energy decorating or remodeling? What outcome do you seek?

Maybe the answers seem obvious to you, but let me probe a little more deeply: Who are you making changes for? What do you hope will happen by making these changes and spending this money? What outcome must be realized for all of the expense, stress, and time to have been worth it? How will you know

you've succeeded? If you haven't really examined—and answered—the important questions before diving into a home remodel or decorating project, you may:

• End up with a beautifully remodeled kitchen that fails to function for your family.

• Start out strong but eventually lose motivation and remain stuck in a cluttered, shabby, dysfunctional home.

• Create a picture-perfect home but realize that nothing has really changed in your life.

When we aren't driven by a clear and internal motivating factor to implement change, the

When we know how we want to use a space and how it should make us feel, we can make informed and intentional decisions about what to buy to meet those goals.

change (if we achieve it at all) rarely lasts. Like a person who loses weight to please someone else or who loses it too quickly and gains it all right back, your house ends up (or stays) out of shape. The answer to "Why should you invest in your home?" is this: You shouldn't! Not unless that investment results in a home in which you feel more carefree, confident, and cared for, and not unless you know why you (not your mom or your sister or your friend) will be happier as a result.

Here's a personal example of a positive life outcome. When I married for the second time, my fiancé and I decided that if we were going to spend thousands on a wedding, we might as well get something long lasting from it (I mean, besides a marriage, of course!). We enjoy hosting parties and barbecues, and we also have a passion for ballroom dance and dreamed of hosting dancing parties and lessons at our home. Inside, our modest house could accommodate, at most, about a dozen people, but outside, our giant weedy-sloped backyard was ripe with potential. We decided to host the wedding at our home and invest in revamping the backyard into a terraced entertaining space. In the year after our wedding, we hosted another half-dozen outdoor soirées, including a zombie-apocalypse emergency planning party and an auction for my local Toastmasters club. That was the prize on which we'd kept our eye the whole time we were neck deep in wedding and remodeling chaos. We stuck with it because we knew we'd end up with an outdoor

space that suited our lives. Visualizing our goal helped us keep perspective and make good long-term decisions. And because we understood our end goal, our why, we ended up with a space that really did enrich our lives.

So how about you? How can you set an intentional goal for your space and project? How can you make decisions for your remodel and have confidence that you are making the right calls? How can you use your home to achieve more joy, calm, love, and success in your life? How can you get—and stay—happier at home?

what do you really want?

With any home project we have to connect to an intention, a purpose, that will serve our life. If you can identify your desires at a core-values level, then you can assess what you need to change to achieve those goals, and then collect the right "tools" to make those goals a reality. For example, not a "new kitchen" but "more healthy home-cooked meals to help my diabetic partner live longer." Or not a "prettier living room" but a "space where I can spend more time with my friends and family." So before you start to redecorate or remodel, you must connect with your core values, see your surroundings with new eyes, and understand how your home supports (or sabotages) the things, people, and activities you most value. Only when you understand the profound impact that your home has in giving you (or keeping you from) the life you crave can you identify how you want to live, come up with a concrete why to guide your successful project, and create a plan to get to your new life.

balance the changes you make to your space

If you are the sole decision-maker in your home, then taking action on the changes you want to make to your space will be straightforward. However, if you are part of a couple, you may find yourself having home remodeling arguments that can seem unsolvable, especially if you are eager to make changes in your home but you're having a tough time getting your partner on board with the plan. You may be tempted to dismiss your partner's opinions, or assume that they don't care about the house. More likely, they just care about it in a different way than you do.

Try to identify how you and your partner see your home. If someone is more of a "nurturer," then the home is a "nest," and reflects how well they care for everyone living there. That might be seen in a desire to have attractive décor that creates inviting, cozy spaces. If someone is more of a "provider" then home is a "castle," offering evidence of their ability to support and protect. That might show up in a home with a solid home value or a trustworthy security system. When you can connect the changes you want to make to the values your partner holds, it will help you have a more fruitful conversation. Remember that while your partner may not express interest in the precise wall color or number of throw pillows, they do care about the house and what happens to it physically and financially. And a

Knowing what you really want helps you filter out well-meant advice that isn't actually a good fit for your life.

kitchen update can be expressed in terms of home value rather than only the social value.

Discover what home means to your partner and then frame the conversation in a way that speaks to those values. You'll get a lot further in your discussions about what to change, how much to spend, and where you both are willing to compromise. Come up with a shared "why" and goal for your space, and you'll spend a lot less time arguing about the size of the sofa, the color of the carpet, or the price of the countertops.

how to use this book

This book isn't an interior design how-to guide. This book is about aligning your heart, your home, and your health. It's about getting a geographical cure (putting yourself in a new environment) without actually relocating. It is about creating a home that will nurture and support the life you deserve to live. If you plan to redecorate, this book will help you identify and buy what you need to feel your best in your space. If you are about to remodel, the activities in this book will better equip you to communicate your needs to an architect, a designer, or a contractor, and will help ensure that you end up with the home, and life, of your dreams. This is important because I want you to have the home of your dreams, not the home of your designer's dreams.

This isn't just a reading book. Treat it as a workbook too. Take a moment to gather these tools (they'll come in handy as you work through the chapters):

• A special notebook or journal dedicated to your Happy Starts at Home™ journey

• Your favorite pen for journaling

• Graph paper for drawing basic floor plans (plain paper will do too)

• Colored pencils or markers

• Your favorite list-making tool (notepad, iPad, phone, laptop) for to-dos, to-considers, and to-stop-doings

As you discover answers about what you need in your living space, put the book down, get up, and make some of those changes. Then pick the book back up and venture onward. I encourage you to read through Chapter I and complete the exercises, which are universally applicable and set the stage for subsequent chapters.

After you've completed Chapter I, turn to any chapter that is calling your name and skip any chapters that don't apply to your life. There is no order in which you have to read the chapters, and there is no magic to doing every last exercise. Each one asks a different question, helping you evaluate your unique situation and discover what you need from your home. With each activity you complete, you'll develop more perspective about your home and be able to see it with new, more objective eyes. This, in turn, will guide you in taking goal-oriented action in your home.

Feel free to use this book on your own, or involve your family. If you are making big changes, perhaps include your partner or kids in the process and have them complete the activities, too. When everyone has a seat at the table, everyone feels respected and heard, and creative solutions often arise. If you're involving your family, first try to do the activities independently and then compare answers. Let it be an opportunity for discovering differences and brainstorming extraordinary solutions. You can even bring in a third party (an architect,

a designer, or a counselor) who is experienced in advising couples if the conversation gets heated. Remember, your relationships are always more important than the color of the carpet.

Okay, let's get started!

Begin to see your home as a tool: use it to get you closer to your goals, and make sure it reflects your values.

happy starts with you:
define your perfect place

Every home is, and should be, unique. Your habits, dreams, family, and hobbies are personal to you, and ideally your space reflects and supports your unique lifestyle. There are no rules for setting up your home; it just has to work for you. In this chapter you will zoom out and get perspective on the big picture of your life so that you can zero in on what needs to change. And throughout this book I will show you how to make those changes without losing precious time, money, and sleep.

For starters, it helps to be aware of the effects that our homes have on our lives. Often we make changes guided by what's trending in popular decorating magazines and TV shows. We try to duplicate what is "right" or current, unconsciously trying to keep up with the Joneses without realizing what is motivating our decisions. But the Jones family may like to host parties for forty people every weekend, while you might prefer to spend a lazy Saturday recovering from the workweek. And really, who cares what the Joneses do with their place? Your home is supposed to make you happy and help you reach your goals!

Simple choices, like hanging your guitar on the wall, set your home apart and make it personal, so that it can never be mistaken for someone else's home.

your heart's desire

Early in my career I worked with a client, Debbie, who was caught in the trap of trying to create the home that other people thought she should have. She showed me pictures of the rooms she admired, then asked my advice about what to buy. Based on her visual targets we identified items that would make over her space to resemble the inspiration rooms, and she proceeded to place the orders. But by my next scheduled visit, Debbie had returned everything and had chosen a different design direction for the room. Now, it can happen that when you actually get what you were asking for it turns out not to be what you want. Knowing this, I wasn't too worried and we went through the process again. However, when it happened again, I put on the brakes: it was time to find out what was going on.

It turned out that every time Debbie had made a decision, she'd asked friends and family their opinions about her new décor. Naturally, everyone had offered different opinions, and because she didn't have a strong internal compass guiding her choices, all those opinions left her confused. Debbie lacked the confidence to say what she really liked. So before we began the decorating process for the third time, we had a heart-to-heart chat.

We explored three important questions: Who did the home need to support? What activities did the home need to support? And how would we know if the work had been successful? The answers to these questions aren't always obvious. At a basic level Debbie's home was a place to eat, sleep, rest, work, and play. That might be factual, but it also doesn't tell us much. In this case the home was for her, yes, but specifically it was for the "grown-up, successful" version of her, trying hard to not need the approval of her family. Debbie and I agreed that her home needed to express her personal identity, and she needed to be comfortable enough to embrace that identity without seeking anyone else's approval. To answer the question "What is my home for?" Debbie expressed that after eight hours or more of caring for other people in her job as a social worker, she longed for a place to recharge so that she could give all that love and energy again the next day. And how would we know her home makeover was a success? If she loved it so much she didn't need her family and friends to love it. It would be a bonus if her family loved it too, but that would be secondary to Debbie liking it on its own merits. Together we set big goals, but with the right mindset and a little help, Debbie discovered they were achievable goals. And very different from just imitating a page in a decorating magazine.

It's important that we clearly define what we need from our home so we don't get distracted by what someone else might want if it were their home.

ACTIVITY 1
the wheel of life:
bridging your wellness and your home

Let's figure out what defines your perfect place, and begin with an exercise that give us a sense of what is (or is not) working in your life right now so we can identify how your home can help. This Wheel of Life activity helps evaluate which areas of your life are working well, and which could use some support, so you can laser-focus your energy and choose changes that will have the greatest impact.

Make a copy of the image opposite. Consider each section and place a dot on the line marking how satisfied you are with each area of your life. A dot placed near the center indicates dissatisfaction; a dot placed near the edge of the circle indicates ultimate happiness. When you have placed a dot on each of the lines, connect the dots. Peaks represent areas of your life that are satisfying, while dips in the circle indicate depletion or imbalance.

You likely have areas in which you feel satisfied and areas being neglected. Did you find any surprises? Many times we "kind of" know the dissatisfied aspects of our lives, but putting it on paper helps us more honestly assess ourselves and our situations.

Take out your journal and make two lists:

• Areas that are full and rich right now

• Areas that are lacking and need attention

This is the starting point for all the ideas we are about to explore in this book. You can use the lists from the Wheel of Life to figure out where best to invest your time and energy to make your home work better for you. Of course, remember that life is never "done": it is organic and eternally shifting. That means your answers will change over time (as will your home) so occasionally revisit your circle to keep tabs on what needs attention in your life.

Now that we have that snapshot of your life, let's discover how you feel about your home.

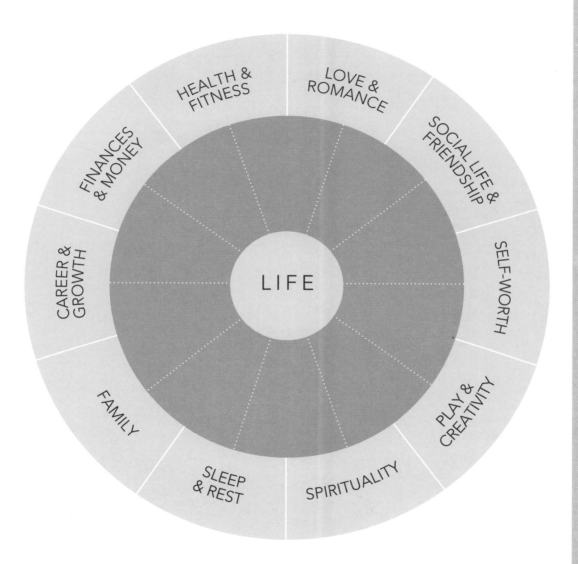

ACTIVITY 2
quiz: how happy is your home?

This quiz will help you think through your level of contentment at home. Answer each question with a rating of 1 to 5, 1 being least like you and 5 being most like you.

① Not at all true, never true, or not at all like me

② Not as true as I'd like, rarely true

③ Sometimes true, half the time true

④ More often than not true, frequently like me

⑤ Absolutely true, always like me, or all the time

When I walk up to my entry door, I start to feel more relaxed.	①	②	③	④	⑤
I find it easy to cook healthy meals at home.	①	②	③	④	⑤
I sleep soundly through the night in my bedroom.	①	②	③	④	⑤
I never apologize for my home when someone comes over.	①	②	③	④	⑤
There are no doors I keep closed to hide the clutter.	①	②	③	④	⑤
Every room in my home is well used by at least one person.	①	②	③	④	⑤
Every person has at least one room that reflects their personality.	①	②	③	④	⑤
I never have trouble finding what I need in my home.	①	②	③	④	⑤
I have plenty of storage space for my belongings.	①	②	③	④	⑤
Everything is in good repair in my home.	①	②	③	④	⑤
I have good lighting for all my tasks in every room.	①	②	③	④	⑤
My home easily accommodates my hobbies and activities.	①	②	③	④	⑤
Nothing in my home makes me feel guilty or sad.	①	②	③	④	⑤
Nothing in my home makes me feel frustrated.	①	②	③	④	⑤
Nothing in my home nags at me "to do."	①	②	③	④	⑤
I feel at home in my home.	①	②	③	④	⑤
It is easy for me to clean my home.	①	②	③	④	⑤
I have a comfortable place for guests.	①	②	③	④	⑤
My home makes me feel comfortable and at ease.	①	②	③	④	⑤
My home reflects my values.	①	②	③	④	⑤

Tally up your score to rate your level of satisfaction and determine if your house is supporting or sabotaging you.

0–40 points

STRUGGLING: Your space actively weighs you down. You may feel frustrated, and you may not feel at home in your house. When you look around you see bad decisions, or your past, or someone else's past. Maybe you feel a sense of failure or maybe the place is just not up to the standards you have set for yourself. You are likely tired of this feeling. You just want to feel calm, peaceful, and proud of your home, but you aren't sure that is possible. You may feel stuck or helpless. Maybe you've set goals to finish a room or get organized, but you're always too busy or too overwhelmed to get very far. You would love a solution, but you don't know where to start.

WHAT YOU NEED: A shift in energy. A vision that will encourage you, empower you, and guide you out of this rut. An understanding that your situation is temporary and changeable. Actionable, small steps that fit into your busy life and create a sense of change and accomplishment. Proof that you are not alone; there is nothing wrong with you; you are not a failure; and you can feel calm, peaceful, and empowered about your home and your life.

No matter where you are at with your home, it's a great starting place. Struggling, Striving, or Succeeding, small changes are within reach that can make your house feel more like home.

41–75 points

STRIVING: Your space has some pluses and some minuses. There is room for improvement, but you are hopeful. Your home feels safe and secure but could feel a bit more welcoming, cozy, and comfortable. You know that you have a good life, but you're never quite relaxed. You are ready to fully love your home and have it work for you instead of you working for it.

WHAT YOU NEED: Clarity around what is working and what can be done to bring you to a more complete place. An action plan to help you finish the incompletes in your home and prioritize projects so you get the biggest impact for your effort. Small but focused steps to make sure your surroundings are working for you and ensuring your success rather than sabotaging all your hard work.

76–100 points

SUCCEEDING AND SUPPORTING: Congratulations! Your home is helping you succeed. You've done the work to create a space that supports you. You regularly donate items that have outlived their purpose, and you don't hesitate to buy things that will bring an element of joy or functionality to your home, because you sense when your home needs a change.

WHAT YOU NEED: More of the same: keep it up! Continue your good habits and occasionally freshen up your space as your life shifts. Since your home is in order, think about where you might be ready to take on bigger challenges in other areas of your life.

"who" is your home?

Your home is so much more than just an impersonal roof over your head. In fact, the personality of your home "lives with you" and influences you as much as the actual people and pets that share your space. That means it's important to figure out just "who" it is you are living with. So if your home were a person that woke up next to you every day, stood in the kitchen each morning when you poured your first cup of coffee, and waited at the front door when you arrived, who would it be? For me, my home is like a best friend who waits for me at the front door with cookies and flowers, and who greets me in the kitchen with a cheery "Good morning." Nice, eh?

It wasn't always that way. After my divorce, my home was more like Eeyore, the somber gray donkey in Winnie the Pooh with a hopeless, defeated outlook and a tendency to remind me of the bad decisions I'd made. After a few months of living with that person I'd finally had enough. I refused to keep living in my past. I wanted my home to remind me I had a bright, exciting, successful future. It was time to toss out Eeyore and invite a new friend into my home. So I repainted the walls, sold most of my furniture, and bought all "new" furniture on Craigslist. Voilà! I was living in a new home, with a new story, and with a new "friend" who could support and encourage me, and help me look toward my future with enthusiasm instead of looking at my past with regret.

Does your home greet you like a cheerful friend, or does it bring you down? Remember, you have the power to decide "who" you live with.

ACTIVITY 3
if my house were a person

Now it's time to identify your home's personality. What does your home say to you?
How does it make you feel? In your journal describe your home as if it were a person that
you know. If you can give it a name, even better. The more you're able to personify the
character of your home, the more easily you'll figure out what needs to change. To help
you frame the conversation, here are some words that commonly come up for my clients
as they describe their home.

- unwelcome
- nosy
- stressful
- self-interested
- pressuring
- busy
- aloof

- shaming
- detached
- crowding
- possessive
- unemotional
- loud
- judging

- messy
- cold
- confused
- disconnected
- demanding
- belittling
- better than me

- pessimistic
- dirty
- uncommitted
- too helpful
- misguided
- embarrassing
- out of control

NOTE: Since most of my clients come to me in a time of lack or when they are stuck, you'll notice these are
mostly negative words. But if you are in a positive place, share those words and feelings freely!

ACTIVITY 4
when it best supports me, my home is like this

Now for the fun part. With whom do you want to live? What would you like to be able
to say about your home? Who would you choose as a roommate? In your journal write
a paragraph as if you are already living in that place. Be sure to write in present tense,
as in "My home is…" or "My home makes me feel…" even though you are dreaming
of a future that may not exist yet.

The future you want is possible. You can come home to a house that makes you happy
and that sends you out into the world full of courage, joy, and love. Of course, creating
a wonderful new life does require clearing out some of the old stuff. Before we can truly
dive into your future, it can be helpful to acknowledge where you came from and
understand how you got here.

What makes a home "happy" will be different for each of
us. Be confident and bold in your choices.

is your home a good housemate?

When you completed activities 3 and 4, were you surprised to discover whom you've been living with? Did you find that your house is like a nagging sister who thinks you never do enough, or maybe a bossy friend who suggests you're lazy, or a well-meaning mother who knows what's "best for you." If so, the only question left is, "Do I really want to live with that person?"

When I made over my house after my divorce, I didn't really make a plan at first. I only knew I refused to go on the way that I'd been living. I needed a change, and in my desperation I didn't care what the change looked like so long as it looked different. At first this resulted in a very unfortunate choice of nearly black paint on my ceiling and a screaming turquoise accent wall in a lime-green room. My room went from "depressed" to "angry"—appropriate, I suppose, since I was practically drowning in anger and frustration and didn't have a guide helping me to see past those emotions. It was just paint, so it didn't matter too much. It got me past feeling stuck. And just by getting unstuck I found some perspective and the ability to take a longer view of where my life was headed. I realized I needed to let myself heal. A couple of weeks later, I painted over the angry-colored walls in a soft shade of pink that created a feminine cocoon where I could be at peace before I headed back out into the scary world of dating and relationships. I'd like to spare you the "angry wall" phase if I can, but know that if you need to create that emotional place for yourself, it's okay. Just try to do it with inexpensive changes: avoid making big, costly alterations like tile, flooring, and cabinets during times of big transition in your life.

You live with your home every day. Make sure it's a housemate you're happy having in your space.

ACTIVITY 5
past, present, future

In this activity, let's look back—physically, emotionally, financially, relationally, and spiritually. Describe the emotional state of your past, your present, and your desired future. In your journal explore the following:

the past: childhood

For each blank, write up to three adjectives that describe how you lived as a child:

- My health was...
- My playtime was...
- Our finances were...
- My faith was...
- I slept...
- I studied...
- My friends were...
- I imagined...
- I felt...
- My parents were...

the present

For each blank, write up to three adjectives that describe how you feel during this present chapter of your life:

- My health is...
- My playtime is...
- My finances are...
- My faith is...
- I sleep...
- I learn...
- My friends are...
- When I daydream I...
- I feel...
- Love is...

the future

For each blank, write up to three adjectives that describe how you want to feel during this next chapter in your life:

- My health will be...
- My playtime will be...
- My finances will be...
- My faith will be...
- I will sleep...
- I will learn...
- My friends will be...
- When I daydream I...
- I will feel...
- Love will be...

Did you notice any connections between your past and present? The path we walk in life makes us who we are, and whether that path is smooth or rocky, as long as we learn from each step we can walk confidently into our future. In this exercise you took a moment to honor the path that led you here, and envisioned your ideal life. Hold on to that vision as you make choices for your home.

Understanding our past and present relationship to home helps us actively set the stage for our future.

ACTIVITY 6
identifying priorities

Your home is a tool for helping you realize your dreams and, as with any tool, in order to use it well it's good to know what you wish to build. With that in mind, let's get even clearer about the priorities you have for your space. In your journal, write down all the wishes you have for your home, as many as you can think of. Then circle three you really can't live without.

If I were to complete this exercise, I might list twenty priorities, but these would be three of the most important:

1. Feeling close to nature, especially trees and birds.
2. Being able to invite an out-of-town guest to stay the night without hesitation.
3. Working from home without distraction.

Complete the activity, then look at your top three priorities. Does your home meet those needs? If not, write down just one change that could get you closer to having a home that aligns with those top three priorities.

If you live with a partner, a spouse, an adult child, or a housemate, make sure you both do this exercise. It is important that you create space for both of your needs to be fulfilled. You may find that you are on the same page, or you may discover that it'll take some work to make sure you're both getting what you need from your home. Please use this exercise to find common ground, not to find fault with the other person's wishes or desires.

A dog-friendly space will have different requirements than a non-dog space. Start with the end goal in mind and you'll have less struggle as you set up your home for your furry friend.

take an inventory

What is all that stuff in your home, anyway? Imagine that I said you could buy as many new clothes as you wanted, but you could never, ever take off anything you'd already purchased. In no time you'd be wearing so much clothing that it would be hard to walk. You'd feel hot and irritable, and be unable to do anything well. That's what the stuff in our homes can be like. If we shop and collect, but never decrease or declutter, the accumulation of stuff is a burden!

Every item rents a space in your heart and in your brain. If there is too much stuff, then you have little room for new fun, new love, or new anything. So let's take a look at what is really in your home. Where did all that furniture, décor, and stuff come from? Why is it in your life, and what purpose does it serve? What feelings are associated with each object?

Sometimes our collections get a little out of hand. Keep what you love, then find a way to show it off so it gets the attention it deserves!

ACTIVITY 7
the happy home assessment

Don't panic—we aren't going to count every last book, pillow, and piece of Tupperware. Instead, we'll start with a Quick Inventory of what is in your home, then go on an Emotional Scavenger Hunt to seek out the good and bad feelings living in your home. Last, we'll reflect on where you are mentally and emotionally with your home right now, and what you want from it when you are finished with this process.

assessment part 1: a quick inventory

• First, choose one room in your home. In your journal list a dozen items in that space. Try to list a couple of big furniture pieces, a few accessories, any gifts, and maybe some semi-permanent features like paint colors or light fixtures.

• Next to each one of your twelve items, write the first feeling that comes to mind when you think of it. Common words can include: nostalgic, poor, happy, rich, sad, frustrated, loved, annoyed, and neutral. Be careful using "neutral." Does that object really have zero emotion attached to it?

• Next, record when you last used the item. "Used" can mean sat on, shared, enjoyed, or worn.

• Now identify who bought or chose each item. Was it you? Your spouse? Ex-spouse? Friend? Mother? Sister? The home's previous owner?

• Finally, note why it was purchased. Was it to solve a specific problem? To make someone else happy? Because you loved it?

For example, here are two items in my living room:

ITEM 1: Hanging chair
EMOTION: Joy and nostalgia
LAST USED: Last night while reading
BOUGHT BY: Me
WHY PURCHASED: Because I wanted a hanging chair like I grew up with at my grandma's home and because I wanted to add some playful whimsy to my living room

ITEM 2: Husband's father's accordion
EMOTION: Nostalgia and sadness
LAST USED: Haven't opened the instrument's case since inheriting
BOUGHT BY: Father-in-law, inherited
WHY OWNED: It's one of the few mementos my husband has of his father

Review your list. Do any themes emerge? Did you buy stuff that you loved at the time but now it makes you feel guilty? Do you have stuff that someone else likes but it only makes you feel frustrated? There is no judgment here, and you'll have your own reasons for what you keep in your home. This is just an opportunity for you to become more aware of your belongings.

assessment part 2: emotional scavenger hunt

Now we are going to do this in reverse, rather like a scavenger hunt. In your journal, list three feelings that you want to get from your home (like warmth, hope, and acceptance) and three feelings you do not want from your home (like pain, guilt, and shame). Take the list and pair objects in your home with each of the six words. Identify who brought that item into your home, and then for the positive feelings the last time you enjoyed/used it, and for the negative feelings why you keep that item in your life.

For example, my positive/negative feelings list might look like:

HAPPINESS: Travel-photo wall—I made it, and my husband and I see it every day when we come home.

SUCCESS: Unicorn sculpture—I bought it for myself to mark my first year in business and it sits proudly on the mantle.

HEALTHINESS: Well-used elliptical machine—My hubby bought it, and it's used three to four times weekly.

FRUSTRATION: Neglected plants in my front yard—I planted them but fail to make time to water properly. I haven't dealt with this because I don't know what else to plant that won't die from neglect and my lack of attention.

GUILT: Family mementos I "have to" keep—My family drove them across country for me and I haven't opened the box in a year. I keep the box because my family's feelings are more important than my need for that space in my home.

EMBARRASSMENT: Too-small dress in my closet with tags still on—I bought it but forgot to return before the return-by date. I still have it because I feel silly taking a brand new dress to a thrift store.

The negative feelings list may seem more revealing than the positive feelings list, but look at both for clues about who or what is in charge of your home. Take a moment to journal your thoughts as follows:

• First, from the positive feelings list, do you use and enjoy those objects? Do you keep them where you can see them, or are they hidden by other stuff?

• Then, from the negative feelings list, what makes you keep the things that cause you pain? Is it guilt for the money you spent? Fear that you won't find anything better? Shame for making a bad decision? A sense of responsibility for other people's feelings? How does holding on make you feel? What would it take to let go?

Things that tell a story of where you've been—and who you hope to become—help create a personal and unique home.

assessment part 3: home exploration

Last but not least, let's evaluate the assets and liabilities in your home. Read and think about the following questions below and explore further in your journal.

- How is my home supporting me right now?

- How is my home sabotaging me right now?

- What goals do I have in the next six months that my home needs to support? How about the next year? Three years?

- How do I feel about my home when people come over?

- How do I wish to feel when people come over?

- What is the main obstacle getting in the way of how I want to feel when people come over?

- Is everything in my home either beautiful or useful?

- What in my home is neither beautiful nor useful? Why is it in my home? If it were gone, what would change?

- What am I holding on to in my space that creates unhappiness? Why am I holding on to it?

- What do I want to create space for in my home and in my life? What would need to go for me to have that?

When you answer these questions honestly, you'll gain a strong sense of what needs to shift in your home as you move forward.

The trick to having a happy home isn't to have a bunch of expensive, matching belongings, but rather to be thoughtful and choosy about what gets to be in your home.

financially fit:
establish an abundant life

What does your home have to do with improving your relationship with money? Everything. To experience abundance in terms of money, belongings, relationships, and time, you need to connect with the meaning behind your money and possessions. Learning to edit what comes into your home, having a say in what surrounds you, and practicing mindfulness around purchases is a surefire way to exercise your abundance and prosperity muscles.

your home and money

Let's look at three ways your home and your wealth are interconnected.

Money scenario 1: money without a life. Your home may be out of alignment with your actual income or wealth. This happens when the stuff in your home makes you feel poor and broke, when in fact you are financially stable. If this is the case, your home may be a barrier between you and great success in your health, relationships, and general happiness.

Money scenario 2: under-abundance. Your financial situation is unsteady, and the balance between income and bills always feels precarious. Your home is full, but your life is anything but abundant. It feels like there is both too much and not enough all at the same time. To make matters worse, your resources are stretched so tightly that you don't feel like you can afford to make changes. If this is you, you are not alone. It is surprisingly easy to feel both overstretched and overstuffed.

An inviting home can make you feel rich even when your resources are stretched.

Money scenario 3: powerlessness. You don't really have too much or too little money, but you have a difficult relationship with money and have trouble asking for what you need. Your home may be bare or it may be beautiful, but either way you may not have had much to do with creating it. If you're disconnected from your home, chances are you're similarly disengaged from your financial planning, too.

money scenario I: money without a life

If you are living out the first scenario, you are financially flush but you haven't achieved the happiness you thought would come with that monetary success. You may have a great job, a position of power, and a life you're generally proud of, but you kind of dread coming home.

There is a huge disconnect between what you wake up to each day and what you are trying to achieve in your life. This can work for a while, but it takes a toll, and if you are building a powerful career and living an energetic life, you need to reserve your energy and make sure every resource you have supports and recharges you. I had a client in just this situation.

My client Derek, a young, attractive, and single man ran his own business, earned his PhD, and owned a beautiful, modern minimalist house. Even with all that success, he lived like a bachelor in an almost cartoonish way: mattress on the floor, bedsheet tacked over the window as a curtain. The place was spare, cold, and unfriendly—the opposite of this vibrant guy. To make matters worse, he had trouble sleeping at night. He didn't want to live like this. He really wanted a "cocoon," a place that felt comfortable, restful, and fun for his friends. After we completed the changes in his home, he experienced immediate success. The day after we finished his bedroom, complete with velvet ripple-fold drapes that enclosed his king-size bed, Derek slept through the night. After the makeover Derek started throwing home parties, and it became a natural place for him to entertain his friends and to recharge before he went out each day to conquer the world.

What does all this have to do with money? Derek had achieved monetary success and felt satisfied in his work. But the dissonance between his successful career and his uninviting house prevented him from feeling content with his home, social,

Our financial success can provide us with a place where we can enjoy the most precious resource we have—our time.

and romantic life. He was holding it together, but once his house felt like a home he didn't need to "hold it together." If you tend to your space and make the changes needed to reflect your hard work and your dreams, each day you'll feel more relaxed and confident,
and in turn discover greater success in your work, love, and health.

money scenario 2: under-abundance

On the other hand, many people (perhaps you?) struggle to make ends meet. Ironically, many people in this scenario lack resources, but find themselves buying new homes, new kitchens, and new organizing systems in an attempt to create a better life—always chasing happiness. Sometimes we end up happier, sometimes we don't. But one thing is certain: when we overspend, we end up less happy.

I regularly help people remodel their homes and create chef-worthy kitchens and spa-like baths, and if it is in your budget and aligns with your goals and values, I say go for it. The problem comes when you don't take the time to figure out the best value for your money and then spend money on things that don't solve the real problem. Any time you are doing something because you feel you "should," a big red flag should go up in your brain. Stop and ask, "Why? Why should I?" "Should" is rarely, if ever, a good enough reason.

Have you ever decided you "should get organized?" Did you go out and buy adorable color-coded bins and labels, and then find yourself so overwhelmed that instead of getting organized, you shoved the new bins and labels into the spare room along with all the rest of the Stuff? That good intention to get organized somehow moved you one step further away from having that charming guest room or dedicated office space. Now you just own a bigger pile of stuff, and it weighs you down even more.

Spending can be important, but spending without focus just drains your resources and increases stress by building up not only piles of stuff, but also piles of debt. Living with abundance is learning how to recognize when enough is enough, and how to spend wisely. Sometimes a kitchen remodel is in order. Sometimes you really can use that amazing organizing system. But oftentimes you really just need to let things go and create new spending habits in order to create a happier relationship with money.

Small rooms and tight resources don't have to be a limitation. Clever problem solving and out-of-the-box thinking can create charming, functional spaces!

money scenario 3: powerlessness

Finally, your relationship with money may not have anything at all to do with how much of it you have. Rather, you may be so uncomfortable thinking about money, or making decisions about money (and therefore your home and other big decisions in your life) that you defer to your spouse about spending and to your boss about your salary. I did this in my first marriage, and I can tell you, it nearly destroyed me.

The thing is, every time we abdicate responsibility about money, our power shrinks and our voice fades. We stop speaking up for what we need, want, and deserve. The great news is that when it comes to your home, you can use it to build your courage and decision-making muscles and have fun at the same time! Why not choose a new wall color for your dining room, something that is just a little scary and stretches your comfort zone? Why not sell that table on Craigslist—the one your sister guilted you into keeping but refuses to take back? Why not take all the kids' toys out of your bedroom and reclaim your grown-up space? If you have spent long enough failing to speak up, even these low-risk actions may feel scary. But as you flex your mini-courage muscles and see that the sky didn't fall, the muscles will grow, and you'll move on to bigger challenges.

Finding our financial voice requires shedding the limits that others place on us, as well as those we place on ourselves. We have to say to our friends, our parents, "Your limits are not my limits." Or "Your fear and scarcity are not my fear and scarcity." As you look at what is in your home you may start to see a reflection of your own fear and shame, and that of your family too.

By letting go of some of the things that hold you down, you also let go of some of the fear.

By taking charge of what is in your home, you start to build your confidence and courage.

Keeping things we inherit honors family memories, but you don't have to hold on to every item. Choose a few special pieces and use or display them proudly.

why do we have stuff?

If we want to have a happier relationship with money and stuff, we have to know where all the money is going, and where all the stuff is coming from. So, where does all that stuff come from? It comes from three main sources: stuff is bought and kept out of fear; stuff is collected and kept out of love. And stuff is kept and multiplied out of habit.

we keep stuff out of FEAR

Sometimes we keep stuff because we fear nothing better will come along. Sometimes we dread the unknown and feel more comfortable with our unhappy but familiar lives. Sometimes we think we are being "prepared." Being prepared is a special trap we fall into, because it sounds so noble. We have a responsibility to be ready for anything. We save boxes for shoes, appliances, electronics—just about anything! When you take a leap and start letting things go from your home, you'll open the door to trust and opportunity. That in turn can help you learn to see life with abundant eyes and worry less about money. So ask yourself, "By keeping this stuff in my house, what fear am I holding on to?"

we keep stuff out of LOVE

Love is a great excuse for holding on. What does love-clutter look like? It looks like the two dozen boxes of photographs and letters that you always meant to scrapbook. Or like the closet full of gifts you meant, but forgot, to give, or the gifts someone gave you that you will never use but that you feel horrible about giving away. Although your impulse to keep these things may start with love, the stuff can still become a burden.

If you find yourself with a house full of memorabilia, gifts, and other stuff that could be categorized as "special," evaluate if you are keeping the stuff because of love, or out of guilt (and if guilt, find a way to let go). Honestly consider if the nostalgia the items bring back are worth the storage, maintenance, and emotional cost of holding on to them. And if that's not enough to help you let go, keep in mind that someday someone will have to go through all that stuff. If you can't do it for yourself, do it for your kids.

It's not so much about how much stuff we do (or do not) keep—it's about keeping a balance and having gratitude for what is in our lives.

Always keep what brings you true joy, but if the things you claim bring you true joy are stuffed in boxes mildewing in the garage, or are piled so deep on the mantle that you can't even see them, reconsider whether those objects really matter. Is the stuff serving you and being honored, or is it just creating a burden for you and those to follow you?

we keep stuff out of HABIT

It's amazing what happens in our lives just out of habit. Habitual patterns are not easily broken, but they are impossible to break if you aren't aware of them. For example, maybe you started saving boxes because you planned to move, and then you got a promotion. It's been ten years, and yet you're still saving boxes. Ask yourself "what have I been holding on to out of habit?"

Having too much stuff gets in the way of you possessing the things you need in your life, and drains your financial (and emotional) resources. If you are suffering from a stuffed but under-abundant life, if you're drowning in clutter but still feel like there is never enough, it is time to create some space. Let go so that you have space to receive, and remember that true prosperity comes from feeling gratitude for all that you have rather than despair over all that you don't have.

If you find yourself feeling jealous of what your friend, or sister, or coworker seems to have, then before you lift a finger to make changes in your home, try to flip your thought process. Start with this: Every day as you put your key in the lock of your front door, say "thank you" to your home. If you have to, tape a note to your door as a reminder to say it as you come in. At first you may not mean it, but say it anyway. Tell your front door, your entry table, your kitchen sink, your living room sofa, "Thank you, I am grateful that you are here to support me." Acknowledge how lucky you are to have each room and each object. Gratitude for even the smallest things counts. Maybe the fact that your key turns easily in the lock is enough to be grateful for. I spent a year of my life feeling angry at a sticky lock, so trust me, a well-working lock is a thing to enjoy!

Our home should be a place where we feel empowered and encouraged to speak up for the little (and big) things we want and need.

find your financial freedom

No matter which money scenario you fall into, making changes in your home can help repair and restructure your relationship with money. Before you move on to the next chapter, take some time with the following exercises to more fully explore your relationship with abundance in your home. Doing these exercises will help you find the clarity to see what brings you satisfaction, the courage to face the music and let things go, and the strength to speak up for what you need from your home, your partner, your boss, and yourself.

An abundant (but balanced) home helps us enjoy the fruits of a fulfilling and happy life.

ACTIVITY 8
money matters

This exercise will help you become more aware of the relationship you have with the objects in your home as they relate to money and your sense of wealth. Complete each statement in your journal:

success-o-meter

An object in my home that I define as "expensive" is...

• That object makes me feel...

• If that object had cost less I would / would not keep it.

An object in my home that I define as "cheap" is...

• That object makes me feel...

• If that object had cost more I would / would not have bought it.

My home does / does not reflect the success I have in my career.

If my boss were to visit my home, I would feel...

If my colleagues were to visit my home, I would feel...

When my friends visit my home, I feel...

When my dates visit my home, I feel...

stuff-o-meter

I have too much / just enough / too little stuff in my home.

There are / are not rooms or closets in my home that are hard to enter because they are so full of stuff.

If I felt better about the amount of stuff in my home my life would be different because…

power-o-meter

I personally chose _____ % of the stuff in my home because I loved it.

The rest of the stuff and colors were chosen by or for...

The things that were not chosen by or for me make me feel...

If there were more of "me" in this house I would feel...

I last made a spending decision in my home...

It was for...

ACTIVITY 9
new discoveries, old habits

Let's explore the ways in which you interacted with abundance as a child, the ways in which you spend now or feel you ought to spend or save, and the ways in which you might start to relate to abundance. In your journal, write three adjectives that best finish the following statements. There are no wrong words.

WHEN I WAS A CHILD:

Money was...

Gifts we got were...

Gifts we gave were...

We bought important things...

We bought fun things...

We were told to spend...

The things in my room were...

AT THIS TIME IN MY LIFE:

Money is...

Gifts I get are...

Gifts I give are...

I buy important things...

I buy fun things...

I spend...

The things in my home are...

IN THE FUTURE IN WHICH I WANT TO LIVE:

Money will be...

Gifts I get will be...

Gifts I give will be...

I'll buy important things...

I'll buy fun things...

I'll be able to spend...

The things in my home will be...

What we see as "expensive," "valuable," "special," or "normal" is shaped by what we had in our homes in our early years.

ACTIVITY 10
taking action

Now that you've completed Activity 8 and Activity 9 what have you discovered about your relationship with money and the ways your home affects it? What three things would you like to change? What resources do you need to make those changes? By what date could the changes happen? What is the very first small, tangible step you can take to make progress today?

Take a moment with your journal and write out a commitment to change. Be specific, clearly spelling out not only the the change you'll make, but also the date by which it will happen, the resources that you need. Finish by identifying one small step you can take today.

Example: *I commit to freshening up my entryway by the end of the month. I will need to buy paint for the front door, and a new entry mat, plus spray paint to freshen up the house numbers. I can start today by changing the burnt-out lightbulb in the porch light.*

Our childhood experience of "home" influences what feels like "home" as we become adults and create our own spaces.

healthy and well-rested:
discover the geographical cure

Every year losing weight and getting fit ranks in the top five New Year's resolutions.
If you're one of the many people seeking a healthier lifestyle, there are countless ways
your home can help you achieve that goal. In fact, modifying your physical environment
can be one of the most effective ways to change a habit and break free from self-
destructive patterns. If you've been struggling for years to sleep better, exercise more,
stop smoking, or change some other behavior, adjusting your physical environment
might be the element that finally tips the scales and makes all your effort pay off.
A so-called "geographical cure" puts you in a space that changes the cues you've been
getting that support your negative habit. What if a simple thing like changing your
kitchen paint color could wake up your subconscious and override any thoughtless
habits you have formed?

The important thing to understand is this: If you are ready to transform your habits
and change your life, not redesigning your space can actually sabotage your best efforts.
In your old space you are constantly cued to keep your old habits. In your "new"
environment you're no longer surrounded by all those reminders. You are free to
create a new reality for yourself!

When we set goals toward being healthy and well-rested,
it's important that our spaces help us reach those goals,
rather than sabotage our success.

short-circuit old patterns and build new habits

It should come as no surprise that it is hard to stop smoking or drinking when you keep finding yourself in the same situation in which you used to drink or smoke. Like Pavlov's dog, you see, hear, and smell the cues and then salivate for the reward. You must change what you sense around you in order to short-circuit the system and rewire your brain for a new way of behaving. Does that mean you have to physically leave your home and move to a new neighborhood? Not necessarily. You can create a space that will send new signals to your brain—and therefore transform your daily patterns—just by making changes to your present environment. Remove as many obstacles as you can, and you will exponentially increase your chances of success. When you eliminate the things that trigger old habits, it's easier to make healthy choices. If you are ready to pursue a healthier lifestyle, why not make your home a participant in (rather than an obstacle to) your success?

By their very nature habits are unconscious. If new healthy choices are a priority, make changes in your home to make your patterns conscious again. Important: Make your choices conscious instead of unconscious. Do this for at least twenty-one days. It takes that long to build a new habit (or break an old one).

get a move on

We all know we should exercise more. Nonetheless, most of us are in the habit of hitting the snooze alarm in the morning, and then at the end of the day trudging to the fridge instead of jogging to the park. If better health is a priority for you, set yourself up for success by transforming the visual and physical cues in your home. Any visual or physical cue that jogs your attention and compels you to make a decision, rather than act on habit, will work. For example, one of my clients wanted to reduce her TV-watching time, so we swapped the position of the sofa and loveseat in her living room—sitting in

Creating kitchen workspaces we enjoy encourages us to cook at home, making it easier to reach our health goals.

a new location, and having to think about where to find the remote, woke up the choice-making part of her brain, freeing her to be more intentional about turning on the tube.

In addition to creating new visual cues in your home, make sure your tools are readily accessible. If you have home gym equipment, remember that it is not any good if you don't use it. If you stick the treadmill in the darkest, dankest corner of your basement, will you really go down there? If you aren't using your equipment, sell what you've got and find something that will work. Never waste precious home real estate on useless equipment. It will just make you feel bad and sabotage your health efforts.

The small tools (running shoes, workout clothes, yoga mat, and the like) are just as important. Can you find your running shoes, or are they buried in the coat closet? When you wake up to rain, do you have a ready-to-grab hat and jacket nearby? Clear out that coat closet and put back only the things that are essential for your healthy-living habits. Finally, clear out your workout clothes drawer. The clothes should all fit, and they should all make you feel good. Your exercise clothing drawer should be so organized that you could get dressed in the dark and feel confident that you'll be leaving the house in a top, bottom, and socks that are in good repair and fit well.

Change up what you see, get your tools in order, and get ready to build new habits.

Even fun, artful choices around the house can speak to our values and keep our goals at the forefront of our minds.

cook up some new eating habits

The more you move your body, the healthier you'll feel, but when it's time to eat, slow down, relax, and enjoy. Let's talk about ways to make cooking at home easier so you have time to sit down and savor what you've prepared. If healthy eating is your goal, then just like with your easy-to-grab workout clothes, you need a kitchen that is easy to use. Clear out the kitchen so you can easily choose and prepare healthy food, and create spaces to eat where you can focus on food and family, not on the TV or other electronic distractions.

Start by clearing the clutter from the cabinets and the counters. Get rid of what you don't need. Begin with the obvious—the stuff that doesn't belong in your kitchen in the first place, such as the junk mail and the art projects. Then get brutal about the kitchen "toys," including the juicers, dehydrators, mandolin slicers, and the like. For now, box it all up, store away, and put a date on the calendar two months from now. If, by that date, you have not retrieved and used an item, donate it to charity. Meanwhile, stick to the basics: Learn to use a decent chef's knife, a paring knife, a skillet, and a soup pan. Add to that a colander and a chopping board, and that is enough to cook almost any healthy meal you can conceive.

Once you have the kitchen in working order (probably by clearing out 50 percent of the stuff), create a peaceful, gadget-free space in your home where you can eat meals. It may sound obvious, but start with a comfortable table and chairs. By banning the distractions you'll be aware of what you are eating and pay attention to your body as it tells you when it is full. You end up eating less and enjoying more.

a remodeling remedy

Sometimes these small changes—clearing the clutter, reducing kitchen equipment to only the essentials—are all that's required to make healthy cooking easier, but sometimes a more dramatic change may be in order. A remodel that results in an easy-to-use kitchen can make healthy-eating goals so much more achievable! If you do take on a remodel, it is important to map out your long-term goals as part of the project so that you don't end up with just a pretty kitchen that isn't actually more functional for you. And remember, you still have to do the work of clearing out the tools and food that sabotage your long-term goals.

If you're serious about having a healthy lifestyle, do what it takes to create functional and pleasant spaces that help you pause and enjoy a distraction-free meal.

destroy the daily stressors

Along with making it easier to exercise regularly and cook healthy meals at home, try to reduce the stressors lurking in your space. Stress causes physical pain, leads to comfort eating, and disturbs sleep, so reducing it will improve everything in your life.

Let's start with something you can pretty easily take control of: working your way through that household to-do list. Fix the broken doorknob, repaint the shabby front door, repair the dripping faucet. Stress makes people sick, and incomplete tasks create unconscious stress. Unconscious stress not only makes it feel like you never have permission to rest, but also takes a toll on your energy and coping skills so that when you need to address a big stressor in your life, you don't have the reserves left to handle it well. So get rid of every little stress that you can. Complete just one home repair a week, and within a month you'll find yourself feeling calmer and more in control of your emotions and home life. Make it a habit to regularly address the small home maintenance needs around the house—burnt-out lightbulbs, dirty walls, dishwasher drips. Trust me, if you tend to them while they are still minor, no-big-deal issues, they won't become a big deal. Why live with broken windows, dusty blinds, and frayed welcome mats? Small fixes, big relief!

For most of us, that home to-do list also includes decluttering or getting organized, and this is a very important part of feeling less stressed at home. Clutter, even when stuffed out of sight in closets and garages, takes up space in our brains and adds bulk to our lives, pulling us down, making us feel less capable, and can lead to habits of overeating, under-sleeping, and couch-potato-ing. Which leads me to the importance of sleeping well.

A home that is in good repair and has a place for everything isn't just for impressing people. It's also a way to reduce the number of stressors in your life, leaving you energy for other, more important things.

rest and renewal through sound sleep

Without sleep, rest, and renewal, none of the other pursuits listed in this book—financial well-being, creative play, healthy relationships—are even possible. It's The Most Important Thing. Without restorative sleep and rest, life becomes unbearable. Everything feels hard. Life just sucks.

On the other hand, when we are rested, we are able to focus and accomplish more. We are energetic, positive, and powerful. We are more generous, kind, and tolerant. We have more patience, less brain fog, and a sense of well-being. One simply cannot overstate the power of restful sleep. And not just sleep. Rest doesn't just happen at bedtime. There also has to be downtime during the day. In our Go! Go! Go! world we often forget to simply breathe, to just be. All that constant running around wears down our ability to cope, and to handle the Big Things when they come along. So while we are about to explore creating a bedroom that allows for deep sleep, remember to create multiple areas in your home where you can just relax, spaces that ease the burden of the day.

the value of a good night's sleep

Of course, it's important to have a relaxing home, but we do literally need regular, restful, complete nights of sleep. Insomnia is a miserable condition, and while sometimes you may need the intervention of western medicine to reset the chemistry of your body, the design of your bedroom can impact your ability to sleep well. There are three main areas over which we have direct influence in our bedrooms: the amount of light and noise, our emotional associations, and meta-messages (the underlying information you receive from a room). Let's address those now.

There are plenty of stressful things in life to keep you up at night—make sure your bedroom isn't one of them.

the power of the dark side

Our bodies are designed to respond to light and darkness as cues for being awake and asleep, but the modern age tends to mess with that natural clock. Luckily, the same interior lighting that has overridden our natural sleep habits can also be used to reset our sleep schedule. Even if you face a busy city street with bright lights, rumbling traffic, and blaring sirens, you can hang some felt-lined blackout drapes which can provide amazing sound-softening and light-deadening effects. Blackout drapes don't have to be expensive or custom-made: a sturdy rod and a pair of off-the-shelf drapes can be plenty.

Try blocking out the streetlights for bedtime, and then consider putting a soft light (something very low, about the brightness of a single candle) on a timer so that it comes on a few minutes before your alarm goes off. That subtle brightening of light will serve as a natural alarm, and you may even find yourself feeling awake by the time the alarm sounds. As soon as you wake up, open the drapes to let in the daylight, and you'll be using your body's natural rhythms to foster good sleep. If short winter days or a nighttime work schedule mean that there is no daylight when you wake up, turn on several bright lamps after you get out of bed to simulate that daylight effect.

You can also influence your sleep patterns through the position of your bedroom in your home. Maybe your bedroom faces west, but you struggle to get up in the mornings, even on the brightest summer days. Try sleeping in an east-facing room for a couple of weeks and see if that makes a difference. Or, if your schedule requires late nights and you need to sleep later, try the western side of the house and make good use of blackout drapes.

Just like pulling the blinds and dimming the lights helps kids nap in the middle of the day, and opening the blinds and turning up the lights helps them wake up again, controlling the lighting in your home can help you sleep soundly and wake refreshed. It's as true for you as it is for the kids.

anxiety in the bedroom

While light and sound control can help us sleep better, the emotional associations you have with your bedroom can dramatically impede your ability to get a good night of sleep. One of my clients went through a divorce and found it distressing to go to bed in the same

Use light and darkness to your advantage as you create a space that helps you fall asleep, and also helps you wake up rested.

Be aware of what you let into the bedroom both
physically and emotionally, and try to keep the space
an area of rest, connection, and renewal.

room that she had once shared with her ex. As part of her healing, she chose to turn the master bedroom into her home office and the guest room into her bedroom. After she made the swap, she had a much easier time falling into a peaceful sleep.

Even if you are in an established, solid relationship, it's possible that you associate anxiety with your bedroom. Many couples find that the only time they really get together are those last moments of the day as they crawl into bed, and so that is when they end up having intense conversations about money, debt, the kids, his mother, her sister, and whether he should quit his job. If those conversations are fraught and argumentative, the couple may unconsciously associate anger, frustration, blame, and other anxiety-inducing emotions with the bedroom. If this is happening in your home, try to carve out some time together earlier in the evening. Maybe pause for a cup of tea together in the kitchen just to clear the news of the day, and agree to stop the conversation before you head to bed. Take "never go to bed angry" a step further, and try never to enter the bedroom angry, either.

voices in the bedroom

Besides light and noise and negative associations, the meta-messages in your room can also potentially disturb sleep. A meta-message is the underlying information you receive from a room. On the surface, it's a bedroom. But the room's implicit message might be that you are sleeping in a workroom, storage room, or toy room— which, in turn, comes with the expectation that you should be addressing the work, the to-do list, or the kids. So what is your bedroom saying to you? If it is filled with paperwork, old magazines, junk mail, kids' toys, piles of laundry, unpacked boxes, and the bed you once shared with your ex, your bedroom is probably sending you these messages:

• You have no time for sleep and should feel guilty for not getting some of this stuff done.

• You don't deserve rest and are not worthy of a place for rest.

• You are stuck in your past and won't ever be able to move on to new and wonderful things.

Wow! And you expect to get a good night's sleep listening to all that garbage? If this is you, it's time for a clean sweep. Banish everything that is unrelated to sleep or sex. Remember, without sleep, none of the other Good Stuff in life is even possible. But with a good night of sleep you can conquer the world!

waking up refreshed

Clearly it's important to go to bed in an environment that encourages and promotes good sleep. It is just as important to wake up to a positive and happy space. If the first thing you see each day makes you smile and eases you into the day, it's much easier to start out on the right foot.

Perhaps you are trying to develop a habit of gratitude, joy, and meditation. Why make it any harder on yourself by having a room filled with obstacles? Put a generously sized nightstand by your bed so it's easy to set down your water glass without a precarious balancing act. Fix the closet door so you don't have to struggle with it first thing in the morning. Repair the sink faucet so the water doesn't drip. You may not be able to control what will happen that day, but if you keep your bedroom and bathroom in good repair, and create a soft, sensual, even flattering environment, you won't be wasting your energy first thing in the day, and you'll find yourself more well-equipped to handle the challenges life will throw your way.

> Your bedroom is the first place you see every morning, setting the tone for the rest of your day. Fill it with things you love.

ACTIVITY 11
bedroom eyes

It's time to look at your bedroom with new eyes. In your journal create a list of all the items that are either 1) unrelated to sleep or sex, or 2) broken, shabby, or leftover from an old relationship. Eliminate at least three items that are unrelated to sleep or sex: toss, donate, or move them elsewhere in your house. Make a plan for repairing what is broken, and, if possible, immediately get rid of anything that evokes past relationships.

NOTE: I realize it's not always practical to get rid of an entire set of furniture leftover from a past relationship. At least toss the sheets—stat!—and replace them with the most luxurious sheets you can afford right now.

ACTIVITY 12
put the "om" in home

No one but you (and your partner) can decide what kind of refuge you need in your bedroom. If you have a high-stress, high-intensity job (including child-rearing) you might need a spa-like, tranquil bedroom. If you have a low-key, even boring and under-stimulating job, you might want to infuse your bedroom with deep sensuality and passion. Your home, especially your bedroom, should be an oasis that meets your needs. As long as the end result is a space where you feel restored and where nothing is demanded of you, you will have been successful. Go to happystartsathome.com and try the free guided meditation to help you visualize your perfect, most supportive space. Once you have listened to the twenty-minute meditation, come back and journal on what you discovered during that quiet journey.

Rather than looking at what other people are doing with their space, try to look within to figure out what you need from your home.

a healthy home is a happy home

Your home environment is the essential foundation to your health and well-being. The great news is that no matter where you live, whether a mansion or a trailer, you can shape the space in a way that benefits you and helps you change destructive habits. The impact of our spaces simply can't be dismissed. It has been well studied in hospital environments that the physical space impacts our ability to heal after our health has been compromised. If it's true in hospitals then it's true in our home, so let's use that knowledge to our advantage, long before we are in crisis!

a safe home is a happy home

The final element to discuss when it comes to being healthy and well-rested is our need for security and safety. In psychologist Abraham Maslow's hierarchy of needs, safety and security is second in line only to our basic physiological needs of food, shelter, and breathing. The stress of feeling unsafe, insecure, or out of control can take a serious toll on your health and on your family's health. This can be especially important after big changes like divorce, a major illness, or the death of a family member. A sense of safety can also be disrupted by a home invasion or a robbery. Literal physical safety in your home contributes to your health and well-being. It's important to make sure you have a home that contributes to a sense of security and safety, stability, and permanence.

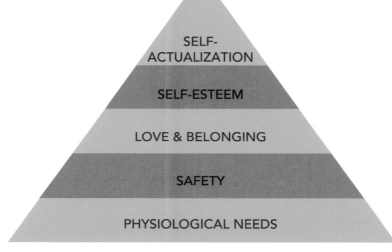

ACTIVITY 13
on guard: creating a sense of safety and permanence

Take a quick assessment of your home using the following checklist:

safety:

• My windows and doors have secure and easy-to-use locks.

• My windows have easy-to-operate shades or drapes to maintain privacy at night.

• My windows and doors are easy to open in case of a fire or an intruder.

• I can see who is at my door without opening it.

• I know the names of my neighbors and how to reach them in an emergency.

• I have checked the fire alarms in my home and have fire extinguishers near heat sources.

• I know where to find the shutoff for the water and gas.

• My family has an out-of-the home, agreed-upon gathering spot in case of emergency.

permanence:

• I know when the people in my house plan to leave and return home.

• There are no unpacked boxes in my home suggesting we might move at any time.

• There is art and other décor hung on the walls, indicating we plan to stay here.

Once you complete Activity 13, note the elements that you were not able to check off and create a plan on the calendar for how you will address each one. Before moving on to the next activity or chapter, accomplish at least one task. I promise you'll feel better when you take action!

ACTIVITY 14
a happy and healthy you

Now that you've read this chapter, what three things would you like to change to be healthier and more well-rested? What resources do you need to make those changes happen? By what date could the changes happen? What is the very first small, tangible step you can take to make progress today? Take a moment with your journal and write out a commitment to change:

A CHANGE:

Date this will happen by...
(both a date I'd like and that is achievable)

Resources I need...

A step I can take today...

The happiest homes let us put down our guard, relax, and breathe easily, freeing us from anxiety and worry.

friends:
inviting places for social gatherings

In today's world we tend to be oversocialized yet underconnected. We have hundreds of online "friends," but many of us feel that we lack close friendships, people who love you enough to give up a weekend to help you move or stop by for a slow cup of tea. If you are lacking a rich social life and meaningful friendships, and wish to have more connection in your life, your home can help, but only if you feel proud of your space. If your home embarrasses you, then it's actually an obstacle to your social goals.

No one likes to feel ashamed of where they live, but when our homes don't measure up to the messages in magazines and on TV about how we should live and what our homes should look like, it can make us feel apologetic. I say save your "sorry" for when it matters.

Not getting the living room vacuumed isn't a sin, and not having the guest room look like a perfect bed-and-breakfast isn't an insult to your guests. What is a problem is the shame that you feel. Why? Because shame puts a barrier between you and your visitor. You try to pay attention to your guest, but part of your mind is fixated on the cobwebs on the lamp and the cat hair on the chair. That kind of embarrassment keeps many people from having guests over at all. They put off inviting people over until the house is "better," "cleaner," or "done." Let's acknowledge that a house is never "done." It is as organic as we are, always shifting and adapting. Any space that isn't evolving is stagnant, a museum. That said, it is important that you get it to a place where it helps you build a fulfilling social life.

Keep things casual and easy so you can focus on the things that actually matter.

an invitation to socialize

A space that invites, rather than prevents relationship building, should look presentable enough for you not to feel embarrassed by it. It should feel comfortable enough to linger in. It should feel so much like "you" that when you leave the house to go out and socialize, you have a clear, unshakable sense of who you are. And it should make you feel safe and secure.

emptiness as an obstacle

Some people avoid inviting friends over to their home because the space isn't decorated—it feels cold, empty, and uninviting. One of my clients, a beautiful young woman in her late twenties, went through a major life shift when she divorced. She bought a condo, excited to launch her life as a newly single person. But soon after, she found herself stuck in a cold white-walled box with a beige couch and metal mini-blinds on the windows—not at all the new life she imagined for herself. Not only did she feel disinclined to make new friends and invite them over, but she also hardly wanted to be in the new place herself. This home was in no condition to support her goal of starting over romantically or socially. She reached out for help, and together we used color and accessories to transform the space into one that felt alive, youthful, and ready for adventure. In no time she found herself making new friends and inviting them to hang out at her place. We hadn't changed her social skills; we just eliminated an obstacle standing in the way of her goals.

abundance as an obstacle (or, the curse of clutter)

Your home can also prevent you from entertaining when you are embarrassed not by its emptiness, but by its clutter. Clutter seems to breed clutter, and before you know it, you can be neck deep. There are many books on cutting clutter, and a lot of people who can help. When I personally work with clients to eliminate clutter, I make it pretty clear that I am not there to be an "organizer;" I am there to help lighten the load. Just labeling the clutter and moving it around will rarely create long-term change in the house—it requires letting go.

Creating a clutter-free, more inviting home can produce surprising results. One of my clients, James, had been laid off and suffered from depression. His wife, Leslie, tried to cheer James up by surprising him with a big-screen TV. Once the TV was installed in the living room, however, it became a huge eyesore. Leslie called me to integrate it into their tiny bungalow living room. As soon as I arrived, I could see that the main problem wasn't the TV: it was the overabundance of furniture. The space overflowed with the furnishings of two living rooms and sagged under all that weight.

Together we decluttered and donated carloads of stuff, rearranged the room to make the most of the remaining furniture and the big TV, and, of course, painted the room a cohesive color to tie it all together. It turned out that this basic makeover helped James emerge from the fog of his depression. Later he told me that he had felt lousy about the house, and it just added insult to injury to be both unemployed and embarrassed by his home—two signs of his "failure." The transformed living room looked like it belonged to someone successful and made James feel like he could have people over and be proud of the space. Welcoming friends into their home helped both James and Leslie rekindle social connections, an important part of battling depression. Even better, the success of the living room transformation led to a home office update, providing James a space in which he could start his own business, helping complete his emergence from his situationally-induced depression. Beautiful!

Settling into our spaces creates a sense of permanence and lays a foundation on which we can make longer term decisions for our lives.

facing shame head on

If you say you're embarrassed by your home and want to change it so you can invite friends over, but you resist making changes, you might want to dig a little more deeply and ask yourself if you really do want to create solid friendships. Houses gain weight the same way people do, and sometimes it happens because we are creating an unconscious barrier to protect ourselves from getting hurt. We say we want to invite friends over, but we avoid making the changes that will let that happen. We use the house as an excuse, because it is safer to stay behind our walls, protected within our fortress, in a place where we can't actually be hurt.

bringing cozy back
(or, how to actually decorate an inviting living room)

Assuming you don't really want to hide behind your walls, how can you create a home that feels natural and comfortable? Another client, Allie, owned a fabulous home with one of the most playful living rooms I'd ever seen. A tomato orange fireplace; sleek gray, low-profile mid-century couches . . . it just felt like a party. Still, she was frustrated because no one ever used it, not even her, and she really wanted a space where she and her friends could, and more importantly would, hang out. As we evaluated what to change, we figured out that her very tailored, stiff couches, lined up like benches, forced guests to face each other, almost as a direct challenge. And two square metal coffee tables were set diagonally so that sharp points angled toward the couches. Everything in the room was fun and colorful, but not a thing in the room was inviting or friendly.

Once we identified why the room felt so unfriendly, Allie and I used the following design guidelines to reinvent the space and create an inviting living room. You can use them too:

1. **Invite comfortable conversation through the seating arrangement.** It should give people options, letting them sit facing each other, side by side, or at 90 degrees to each other, depending on what feels right at the moment. Think of a fire pit, the feeling of folks gathered around a campfire. Avoid having the furniture all lined up like a hallway or a waiting room, or all facing a big TV.

Simple design guidelines, like arranging furniture in a way that makes it easy and natural to chat, can have a huge effect on how we experience and use a space.

2. Create easy movement and flow. Make it simple to enter and exit the room, ideally by two paths or at least a generous space. Leave at least three feet between pieces of furniture or walls that create a "hallway" or path. Avoid sharp angles intruding into the paths, and use round coffee tables when needed to create flow.

3. Keep it human-scaled. Avoid giant pieces of artwork towering over the room cathedral-style, and consider softening huge picture windows with simple drapes that gently frame the window. As much as possible, create nooks for intimacy—like quiet conversation and reading.

4. Make it touchable. Make generous use of soft throw pillows and blankets. Avoid anything that is unpleasant to touch or feels too delicate and off-limits to touch. Use feather or feather-like pillow inserts so they mold to your body instead of bouncing you off the sofa.

5. Make it approachable. If your guests feel like they have to be too careful, they'll never be at ease. Avoid a lot of glass, white fabric, shiny metal, or delicate objects of art.

6. Light it up. Layer the light by combining overhead lights with floor and table lamps. Adjust lighting based on the activity in the room: Brighter light makes your older guests more comfortable; lamplight is warmer, easier to control, and more flattering for everyone. Avoid having your only light source come from overhead or recessed lighting, because overhead lights cast deep shadows under the eyes. When people feel attractive, they are naturally more at ease.

7. Consciously choose your wall colors. Bright orange may be fun, but a sharp tangerine might be a little too forceful in its playfulness, practically screaming at your guests to enjoy themselves. A spiced pumpkin like Benjamin Moore's Buttered Yam might be a better choice. Or paint the walls a neutral color and bring in fabulous colorful accessories.

Friendly colors, touchable textiles, and flattering light all
help create a living room in which guests will want to linger.

feeling "at home" makes it easier to make friends

Having a home you feel proud of affects your social life at every age. Just like the way a feeling of safety and permanence affects our health (see Chapter 3), the feeling of permanence and belonging affects our desire and ability to form friendships. We are naturally more willing to connect when we know we are staying put. Conversely, when we live half-moved-in, half-unpacked, we increase our isolation. By putting down visual roots, we not only create a place to welcome friends but also feel more rooted and willing to invest in relationships.

Our homes, both literally and figuratively, shape our place in the world. It's where we wake every morning and go to sleep every night. It cannot help but affect how we engage with the world around us. If you are feeling oversocialized but underconnected and want to use your home as a way to fix that, consider hosting a book, wine, or garden club. A regular meeting, once a month, of a few like-minded people over the course of months or years can build genuine friendships and social bonds that are not replicated anywhere else in life! If you can't imagine inviting people into your home, either because you are stopped by emptiness or by clutter, make some changes as soon as you can!

We naturally respond to the energy of the people around us, so creating a room that puts you at ease will help set your guests at ease, too.

Whether you'd rather have twenty people over for game night, or just enjoy a quiet evening with your best friend, make sure your home makes it easy to have the social life you want.

ACTIVITY 15
private vs. public spaces:
map your home's social life

Create a basic floor plan of your home. It doesn't have to be to scale, just make sure each space is represented, including outside decks and gardens. Choose three colored pencils or crayons.

Once you have drafted your floor plan, use one color to mark areas that are considered social spaces and are comfortably used by three or more people. Use a different color to mark areas that are considered personal and private, just meant for one or two people. Use a third color to mark areas that feel uninviting and unfriendly, places that aren't being effectively used regardless of whether they are meant for social or private use.

Look over your colored floor plan. Are you surprised by which areas feel private or intimate, which areas feel social, and which areas feel uninviting? Take a moment to write in your journal about your experience in mapping the social life in your home.

ACTIVITY 16
making friends

Let's assess your social life. Remember that there are no right or wrong answers, and your preferences may differ from others in your family. Maybe you draw energy from quiet moments relaxing on your own. Perhaps you love a good party, but only occasionally. A "good" social life might involve hundreds of people, or just a few close friends. The only cue to follow is your personal contentment level. But if you feel you are lacking in the social and friendship departments, take that as a sign to create change and evaluate how your home can help. If you are content and feel fulfilled in your relationships, don't feel you "should" change anything! In your journal complete the following phrases:

• The last time I had friends over was...

  and it made me feel...

• The last time I apologized to someone for the state of my home was...

  and it was because...

• If friends were to drop by right now, I would feel...

• If my boss were to drop by right now, I would feel...

Based on your answers, take a moment to write about the status of your social life and changes you would like to see in it.

ACTIVITY 17
taking action

Now that you've read this chapter, what three changes would you like to make in your friendships and social life? What resources do you need to make those changes occur? By what date could those changes happen? What small, tangible step can you take to make progress today? Take a moment with your journal and write out a commitment to change:

A CHANGE:

Date this will happen by...
(both a date I'd like and that is achievable)

Resources I need...

A step I can take today...

Whether "being social" means having a couple friends over, or a couple dozen friends over, when our home is party-ready we never miss a chance to connect.

love:

romance, companionship, and starting anew

This chapter isn't about seducing your next partner, or making sure you have flattering lighting in the bedroom (though, on second thought, that's not a horrible idea!). It's simply about making sure your home is doing the job you need it to do when it comes to your romantic life. The design of your home can help keep your love life alive or even bring new love into your life. It can also keep love away. Design that sparks love isn't particularly magical or "woo-woo." It's not about love potions or painting your walls red. It's simply about becoming aware of the messages your home is sending out about how open you are to sharing your space and your life with another person.

Your home is also a place of hope and healing when relationships end and it's time for a new beginning. Love is as skittish as a bird, and like it or not, it never promises to stay. So whatever situation you're in, remember it's just one chapter of your life. Use the information here to turn the end of every story into the beginning of a new one.

Our homes can help us move in and out of love with grace,
letting us create space for others, and space for ourselves.

three basic needs

If you've been reaching for love for years but it remains out of your grasp, take a look around you. Do the messages in your home line up with what you say you want? If you want to bring love into your life, or rekindle an existing relationship, you'll need to do three important things:

1. Know yourself first.
2. Have space that is about both of you.
3. Allow room for change and growth.

loving and knowing yourself

Whether you are just starting out on the road of love, or you've been around the block a few times, you can't be an effective partner for anyone else if you haven't first figured out and embraced your own strength and worth. Your home actually reflects how well you know—and love—yourself.

In the years before you share a home with another person, you have a wonderful chance to create a unique, personal space without the vote or opinion of someone else. Cherish this time. Often we are so eager to move from singlehood into partnership that we miss that wonderful chapter when all the choices are our own and there are no arguments over how to spend money and which paint color to choose. If you are in-between partners, or newly single, take this opportunity to create a personal shelter and make your home a reflection of you.

A happy home should help you say, "I know who I am, what I like, what I want and where I am headed." If you don't establish this kind of home before you partner with someone else (particularly someone who does know what they want and has strong opinions about it), you may find yourself steamrolled by love and either never find your own voice, or one day feel the need to break free from the partnership just so you can sing your own song. Come into the relationship singing your own music and you both have a better chance at success. Shaping your home to fit you perfectly is a part of that journey.

a surprising way to find love

Once your home reflects you, you'll start to feel a lot more settled about being on your own. You'll feel so much more at home in your house that the urgency to share your space may even diminish. Watch out! This is the very moment in which you might get what you asked for (i.e., love).

This happened to my client Hannah. For years she'd wanted to put down roots, get married, and start a family. She had found financial and professional success with a career in law, and lived in an expensive apartment with a water view, but she hadn't met a partner with whom she could see herself establishing a long-term home. When I walked into Hannah's apartment, I couldn't help but notice that nothing about her space suggested she planned to stay put, much less make a lifetime commitment to someone else. She'd been so focused on moving on, she'd never moved in, despite living there for five years! Finally tired of waiting for her proverbial Prince Charming, she called me to help her create a welcoming, feminine space she could call home. When it was done, Hannah loved the space so much that she started not only spending more time there, but also inviting family and friends over more often. The result? Within a year, her increased social circle led her to both meet and marry the man of her dreams. So maybe it is magic?

Being romance-ready starts long before you hit the bedroom. Make sure all your spaces reflect you and your values to help you partner with the right person.

make room for love

Once you've created a space that reflects your preferences, desires, and dreams, it's time to make emotional and physical space for another person. Don't worry, that doesn't mean you have to destroy all the work you just did to make the place your own. You're not decorating for someone else; you are simply creating a little room in your home (and heart) for another person.

send the right message

The home is like a beacon that signals to the world whether you are ready to give and receive love. This is true both when you are looking for love and when you are in an established relationship. To illustrate this, picture the following rooms which send exactly the opposite message (I've encountered all of these over the years as an interior designer).

Rooms that appear to reject romance:

- An adult woman's bedroom stuffed with toy animals and a pink satin comforter on the bed.

- A single guy's bedroom with a mattress on the floor and an old sheet tacked over the window.

- A bedroom with a double bed pushed up against the wall, with every available closet and dresser overflowing with just one person's clothes.

- A well-to-do bachelor's living room dressed to the nines in high-quality furnishings, all in heavy masculine black leather and sharp-edged stainless steel, focused on a massive flat-screen TV.

- A socialite's living room painted pale peach and furnished with a gorgeous white silk sofa, a cream wool rug, sheer linen curtains, and a glass coffee table.

- A couple's bedroom so full of kid's toys, paperwork, and laundry, you'd never know the room was meant for rest and sensuality.

When we are ready to invite someone into our lives it's important that we prepare room for them so they feel welcome and not like an uninvited visitor.

Each of these clients insisted that they were open to love and ready to share their time and space with another person, but their rooms all flashed a big "No Vacancy" sign. A mattress on the floor and a sheet over a window imply that the person living in that room isn't ready to commit to anything that requires thought or investment. A bed pushed against the wall literally blocks the way for another person to crawl into bed, and an overstuffed closet signals "no more room."

If you're preparing for a new partnership, make a fresh start in the bedroom! Pictures of old girlfriends, gifts from old boyfriends, and even mementos of childhood may need to be tucked away if you really are ready to begin an emotionally healthy relationship. Likewise I recommend changing up the wall color and splurging on new bedding if you are coming out of a relationship and want to find new love. If you're staring at your past, then you'll live in the past. Clear it out and make way for a bright and love-filled future.

make room for your new partner

Be aware that once you've invested time and money making your home fit you just right, you may feel resistance to someone coming in and changing it. That's normal. It's also normal for your new partner to be looking around and wanting to make the house feel like their home, too. Of course, if you've fallen deeply enough in love to move in with someone, hopefully you'll be eager to create a space that reflects you both. To get on the same page, work through the activities in this book together, especially in Chapter I, so you can create a shared vision.

Cohabitation works best when both partners work hard to make sure the other person feels at home in the house, no matter if it started out as "mine" or "yours." It is much harder when one person is oblivious to the fact that someone has moved in but still feels like a guest in the house. It's even worse when, like my client Amanda, you get married, move into your new husband's home, and then discover that even though all the furniture and decorations were chosen by his ex wife, he's unwilling to change it because "he spent good money on all that furniture." It took Amanda a while to help her new husband understand that without some changes to the space she would continue to feel

When you find someone to share your life with, use that opportunity to create a home that reflects the unique relationship that only you two share.

like an outsider in her own home. Happily, he did finally agree to make the changes needed to turn "his house" into "their house."

To make blending homes a positive experience, it's important to ask your partner what they need from their home, to listen without judgment, and share what you need with them. Use this book to frame the conversation so that it doesn't devolve into an argument about whether or not we should keep "your chair" or if there is room for "my books." And enlist the help of a design psychology coach if you can't figure it out on your own. If you're committed to creating a home for two, there is almost always a way to achieve that goal.

make room for the love you already have

When we commit to a partner, we commit to compromise and sharing—our feelings, our fears, our dreams, and our sofa. How we share our physical space can be a strong indicator of whether a relationship is a partnership, or a dictatorship. Many couples start off great, creating room for two, but over time one of the partners seems to get squeezed out of their own home. Entire sitcom episodes are dedicated to recliners that are banished along with their owner to the "man cave" once a women takes over, but the joke can quickly go from amusing to damaging. Have you unconsciously turned "our home" into "my home?" If your marital home is perfectly decorated but only represents you, consider what that says about your feelings toward your spouse and what that suggests to the world about his or her place in your home. Consider bringing your spouse back into the space.

Clutter can become a weapon of marriage destruction, too, and can indicate signs of a neglected relationship. My client Beverly said this started in her home when she "borrowed" her partner's home office "temporarily" to store some stuff she was meaning to donate. The little pile of stuff not only never quite left the office, it grew in size. Before long the "office" became nothing more than a storeroom, and her partner no longer had a place for their own creativity and growth. If your spouse has been craving a room of their own, make it a priority to carve out that space. It shows you support and respect them.

When one person has strong decorating preferences it can be easy to steamroll right over the other person. Try to make sure it always looks and feels like you both live there.

make space for making love

Marriage neglect shows up in many rooms in the house, but most commonly it's the bedroom that tends to stagnate over the years. When we put energy into the house, we usually take care of the public spaces (kitchens, living rooms) first. Don't get me wrong: the public spaces are important. They define the family culture, create space for spending time together with family and friends, and help us feel secure and confident no matter what the world throws our way. But the bedroom is no less important, because that is where we tend to our marriage, where we stand together and repair what the world wore down that day. When our bedroom is more about the work we have to do than the love we need to make, when it is filled with toys from the kids, papers from work, and laundry that needs folding, we miss an opportunity to nurture our marriage. You must have a time and place where you are allowed to rest, laugh, and touch, without anything else demanding your time and attention.

Try to make sure the bedroom is a space that strengthens, rather than strains, your relationship.

ACTIVITY 18
setting the stage for love, or rekindling a flame

Are you committed to love and to having a loving relationship in your home? If I were to look in your home, would I believe you? Read through each item listed below. If there are any that don't describe your home, consider what you might want to change:

- I have a bed that is comfortable for two, with two generous nightstands and two easy-to-use, sturdy lamps on either side.

- My bedroom is clearly a room for adults, not for children or animals.

- My bedroom is a room for rest and romance. It is clear of laundry, paperwork, and other distractions from rest and romance.

- My closet and dresser have open space; everything in my closet and dresser fits; and nothing reminds me of my ex or past life.

- My living room has a space that feels comfortable and safe for spending time with another person.

- My entryway is clear of clutter; there is space for visitors to put down their belongings and stay awhile.

- It is easy to shut out the noise and light from the world when I want to retreat into my bedroom and rest or connect with my partner.

- My home clearly reflects who I am but is also flexible and ready for change.

- There are clean towels, fresh soap, and plenty of toilet paper in the bathroom.

- My home is easy to find from the street, with clearly marked house numbers and a safe walkway.

Thoughts? What came up for you here? Take a moment to write in your journal.

one door closes, another one opens...

Love makes us vulnerable, and it doesn't guarantee a happy ending. The painful truth is that opening our hearts to another human makes it likely that we will face the loneliness that comes after a breakup, divorce, or death. When this happens to you, your home can be part of the healing process, and with time, you can emerge stronger and more resilient, able to turn the end of that love story into the beginning of a new one. Let's make sure your home does its job and helps you move forward, rather than holding you back. Remember, your home is just sitting there, ready to help you live a happier, healthier, more successful, and meaningful life. So why not put it to work and allow that support?

where to begin

When you lose the one you loved, either through divorce or death, it rips out your heart no matter what the state of the relationship was before the loss. Even in a messy divorce it's not just the bad stuff that ends, but also the dream you held when you walked down the aisle and said, "I do." Leaving or losing a partner creates a lot of confusion, and it can be hard to trust your instincts or know how to move forward in a healthy way. When it comes to your home, that confusion increases when it's time to figure out what to do with the stuff in your space that reminds you of them and you have to ask two diametrically opposed questions:

• How do I honor the past?
• How do I let go of the past?

If you've experienced the death of a loved one, then it'll probably be obvious why you'd want to honor your history together. If you got divorced, it'll probably be obvious why you want to let go of the past. But every widow has to find a way to honor that past love while still creating a new life, and every divorcee has to find a way to hold onto what they learned from that old relationship without letting the baggage come into the next one.

Memories linger long after relationships end, but your home shouldn't haunt you. Do what you need to in order to make it a place that helps you heal, rather than one that holds you back.

when to let go

You might have trouble letting go of things from your past relationship because they are your memories too. This process will require honesty. When you look at that souvenir from your trip with your ex, do you feel more than 50 percent happy, or more than 50 percent sad? Rarely is that emotion split right down the middle. If you are more happy than sad, keep it—it's part of your past and the path that made you the person you are today. If you are more sad than happy, it's time to create a new memory.

If you really can't decide if an item makes you more happy than sad, put it in a box and store it away. Mark a date on the calendar three to six months in the future, then revisit the item on that date. If you didn't miss it while it was stored away, or if you are overwhelmed with sadness when you unwrap it, maybe it's time for it to go.

Try not to keep anything out of negative emotions like spite or guilt. In the case of divorce, keeping something out of spite means that you are holding onto it post-breakup, not because you care about it but because you know your ex loved it and there is no way you are giving it back. You're a grown up—behave better than that. Guilt shows up when you know that you don't actually want a certain thing in your life, but you either think it "cost" too much to part with (in actual money or in divorce negotiations), or you feel like your lost loved one would want you to keep it. In fact, your loved one would want you to move on and have a happy life. Letting these kinds of emotions dictate what stuff you keep in your home won't help you build a fulfilling future. The objects will remain obstacles to your highest success. Let go.

keeping memories for the kids

Sometimes, it's easy to let go. After divorce, you may want to burn all the memories of your ex to the ground. Even after a loved one passes away, at some point you will likely be ready to create room for new love. In both these scenarios, if you have kids it's your job to hold on to touchstones that they will appreciate when they are older. Later on these touchstones, like a simple birthday card signed by mom and dad, can help them understand that neither divorce nor death changes the love parents have for their kids (even when they may be behaving like children themselves). Find a way to keep these mementos safe for your kids, but also in a way that lets you move forward. A special memory box or trunk can be a nice way to go about this.

When it comes to putting down roots for you and the kids after a loss, creating safe and happy spaces in the home can help them feel a sense of permanence and security in a world that has just turned upside down. That said, while creating two homes post-divorce may require buying new things for yourself and the kids, guard against the desire to compete with your ex. You will never, ever gain your children's affection or loyalty through gifts and material things. It's a losing battle. Don't engage.

As you explore the balance between holding on and letting go, take it one step at a time, and keep this goal in mind: to find contentment, peace, and happiness again.

healing versus hiding

Your home is a good place to heal after loss, but it's also an easy place to hide. I remember how embarrassed I felt after my divorce, and it kept me from reaching out to my friends for support. Try to let your home be part of staying connected to your social network, and invite your friends over. They want to see you.

Be prepared to ride a crazy rollercoaster of emotions. You may feel compelled to make drastic changes to your habits, your home, your wardrobe, or your work. Or, you may feel the need to keep everything exactly the way it was. This may give you comfort and a feeling of security and control. You will have to trust your intuition to steer you to the answers. If you sometimes get it "wrong" (i.e., if you regret decisions later), be gentle with yourself and know that you are only human. It's okay to be less than perfect.

How long it takes to emerge from your cocoon will vary. Only you can say how long is long enough to grieve. But when you're ready, I can say that your home is a great place to dip a toe into the waters of moving on. Whether it's been two months or two years, you can try small steps (repainting the guest room or reorganizing the spice rack) to see how it feels. Don't feel pressured to make drastic changes, but don't be afraid to take a risk, either. You're stronger than you think.

NOTE: It's best not to get involved in a new relationship if you can't quite bring yourself to remove your former spouse's possessions from your home. That can be unfair to your new partner. When you are ready to love again, you'll be ready to make room for that new special person.

Your home can be a quiet place to heal, and also a safe place to try out new ideas as you emerge from a loss. Maybe you haven't been dreaming of a bright pink sofa, but perhaps it's time to try a bold paint color?

ACTIVITY 19
making peace with the past

Whether an old relationship was positive or negative, it's still in the past. For you to move forward, it may be time to close the book on that old story. Walk through your home room by room, and in your journal list any object that reminds you of a past relationship and brings up feelings of sadness, guilt, shame, or embarrassment. Explore how it makes you feel, and how you might feel if that object were either not in your home, or were put in a sacred but out-of-sight place. Find one or two items that feel easy to release, and give them a new home either in a special box in your garage, a closet, or out of your life completely. With each moment of release, express gratitude for the memories you cherish or the lessons you learned, and give yourself permission to move forward into a new chapter.

As you move into and out of relationships, do what needs to be done in order to have a home that honors the past but makes space for creating new memories.

ACTIVITY 20
attract new energy into the bedroom

If you are ready to move on from a past relationship and move into a new one, here are ten ways to freshen up your space and set the scene for your next adventure in love:

1. Flip your mattress.

2. Sleep on the other side of the bed or right down the middle.

3. Move your bedroom to another room.

4. Buy new sheets and pillowslips. Consider a new mattress.

5. Open the windows and clean them inside and out.

6. If you haven't already done so, get rid of any toys (plush or otherwise) or undergarments that your ex brought into your relationship.

7. Repaint the walls and, ideally, the ceiling.

8. Clean it top to bottom, even under the bed.

9. Add more light by changing your bulbs or bringing in a new lamp.

10. Bring in something new—not because your ex would hate it but because you love it.

In your journal note three changes you will make to your bedroom, and commit to taking action by a specific date.

years later: when stuff bubbles up

Letting go and moving forward may or may not happen right away, but at some point you'll have to deal with it, even if it's just because you are moving from one house to another and have to pack it all up. Years after a break up, divorce, or death, it can still be a struggle to let go of the emotional and physical mementos of a past relationship. Sometimes the letting-go process opens up old wounds. Sometimes all that stuff overwhelms you and you don't know where to begin. Even if you became single by choice and you know you're better off without that old relationship, letting go can hurt.

Again, there are no rules. Don't judge yourself too harshly if you aren't moving on at the rate your friends or family think you should. Sometimes it is better to let things settle and see how you feel in a month or two. Sitting with your pain, grief, or confusion for a bit can be okay. Then you can test out small changes in your home to see how it feels to move forward. Sleep on the other side of the bed. Replace the dinner dishes with something bright and cheery. Add whimsical throw pillows to the sofa. Bring in small touches that say "you"—anything that helps you look toward your future instead of your past. It may feel uncomfortable at first because it is unfamiliar. But just because it's unfamiliar doesn't make it bad. After all, hope always comes wrapped in the packaging of the unknown.

Whether you remodel the bathroom, or simply run yourself a bubble bath, celebrate the steps you take forward into the next chapter of your life.

it takes a village:
family identity and the power of play

Our homes are physical representations of our family and cultural identities. What we choose to have around us says a lot about who we are (or at least how we wish to be perceived) and what we value.

As we explore family and see how it relates to identity, know that "family" isn't limited to any one definition. Here, it pretty much covers all the humans and fur-babies living in a space together. That could mean you and the cat, a group of housemates, or the Rockwellian mother, father, and children. In this context, family is about group identity, even if that is a group of one.

The design and decoration of your home doesn't just reflect your family and personal narrative, it also profoundly impacts your family culture. What you have, or do not have, in your home affects how you play and work together, and shapes the "rules of engagement" in your home. How you set up your furniture affects how you spend your time together as a family, where and how you eat as a family, and how you identify both as part of, and independently from, your family. What I mean is that the things in your home not only result from who you are, but also affect who you will become. That means you control the direction of your story. You are not only living it; you are writing it. So write a story you want to read.

Your home is the one place that can be a pure reflection of you and your family. Toss society's concept of what makes a home happy out the window, and create a space that makes you feel great.

values-driven design

I am sure we can agree that a comfortable, family-focused home doesn't need to be expensively appointed, but what are the keys to creating a safe, cozy, inviting home? Start by identifying your family's values and culture, and then build an environment that supports and reflects it. No one can tell you what your values should be, but once you have identified them, it becomes much easier to design around them. Here are examples of some of my clients' values and corresponding design ideas that serve those values:

Value: Spending time outdoors, hiking in the woods, playing outside.

Design: A mudroom with an outdoor entry; easy-to-access storage for outerwear such as boots, gloves, and hats; and easy-to-clean flooring.

Value: Eating together, praying at meals, sharing the day over lovingly prepared food.

Design: A dedicated dining room that is casual and inviting, free from electronic distractions, and close to the kitchen so that setting up and cleaning up create more opportunities for family interaction.

Value: Hosting parties for your community or networking group.

Design: An open-concept kitchen that invites relaxed interaction between the cook and guests, and has easy-to-care-for flooring that is forgiving when it comes to cleaning up bits and crumbs after the party.

Value: Multigenerational living.

Design: A home with spaces that can be personalized for each generation so that no one feels like they are living in someone else's home, are accessible and safe with generous lighting and few steps, and promote both gathering and privacy when needed.

Value: Having conversations.

Design: A living room with furniture that's arranged for easy conversation rather than focused on the TV; adjustable lighting that works for different activities like reading, playing games, or relaxing with a cup of cocoa or a glass of wine; comfortable, easy-to-maintain seating that's free from dog slobber, cat hair, Cheerios, and flat cushions.

Whether you're a world traveler, an avid hiker, a voracious reader, or a music lover, let your home be a reflection of your passions. What does your space say about you?

As you begin to personalize your place, don't put too much pressure on yourself to get it perfect from the start. A happy, unique home develops over time.

don't set yourself up for frustration and failure

The best way to maintain your home and your sanity is to understand your family culture and work with the habits of the people living in and visiting your home. If you have a rambunctious family with teens and dogs constantly coming in and out, installing white wool carpeting will just invite disaster. If you regularly host foodie parties and guests wander your home holding plates of red sauce and glasses of red wine, reconsider that $10,000 silk and wool rug. If you really prefer gardening over dusting, think twice before you install glass shelves to display your grandmother's figurine collection. Design with your family and lifestyle in mind, and create peace.

personalize your place

If you're new to decorating, you're unlikely to achieve a developed, rich, personal feeling on your first try. Even if you hire a designer to accessorize with delightful, whimsical treasures, it still won't feel as warm and personal as it will when you collect items over time. It's great to finish the house enough that it feels done, but think of some elements as placeholders, and then let yourself play over the years. Collect a bag full of seashells from your day at the beach, pour out the generic ornaments that your decorator put in the glass jar on your mantle, and refill it with the shells that now tell a story in your life.

If you're a seasoned decorator, take a walk through your home and explore the stories that are already present. Visit each room and think carefully about how each object makes you feel. Some will evoke pleasant, positive memories; others will bring up guilt, frustration, even shame, fear, or sadness. Others maybe "should" be meaningful but really are no longer important to you. As you go through your space, you'll probably associate stories with each item you see—some happy, some sad, some bittersweet. Of course, just because an item has a story doesn't mean you're stuck with it or have to keep telling yourself that story. If it's time to move on, do so! And if it's someone else's burden or debt or shame you are keeping in your home through that object, let it go. Why would you hold onto someone else's shame?

honor the past, embrace the future

How we handle the stuff in our houses creates an important lesson for us—and for our kids.

Some people keep everything and end up with a house stuffed so full that nothing has meaning. Overstuffed homes can be suffocating to the point of embarrassment for everyone who lives there. Guests might not be invited over or, if they are, apologies are made for the state of the house. Every interaction is tinged with shame. When you keep everything, sure, it means there is no risk you'll get rid of anything you care about, but it also means bad, unhelpful stuff lingers in your home, the past is never permitted to go away, and there isn't room for anything new. You could bring in a beautiful new reading chair, but where the heck would it go? Crammed next to the ratty recliner and shredded cat tree?

On the other hand, a perfectly curated home can be just as distressing as a too-cluttered home. I see this in homes where folks are so brutal about getting rid of things, or about keeping out anything that doesn't "match" the house, that nothing is ever permitted to grow in meaning. "Perfect" spaces often feel generic, no matter how beautiful they are, rather like a hotel room. It's an uncomfortable way to live, and creates an environment where everyone must be constantly alert and careful. Heaven forbid something got damaged! Extremely minimalist homes have a similar problem—the space can feel sterile, cold, and uninviting, a lot like you never moved in. This kind of passing-through existence can lead to a difficulty in setting down roots, forming long-term relationships, and building trust with new people.

Surround yourself with things that have meaning, and let each person in the home contribute to the family story. At the same time, remove things that aren't serving you, even when those things were given to you by family. Blood may be thicker than water, but that doesn't mean you have to hold onto all your family heirlooms. We have the right and responsibility to decide what lives in our home, and while people with very good intentions may think you really could use their old furniture, if you don't need another sofa, then you are inheriting a burden, not a gift. The key is to find a balance between keeping what is meaningful and eliminating what is not.

When memories are hidden away in boxes we miss a chance to integrate family stories into our everyday life. Thoughtful displays can give us a beautiful foundation on which we can build a future.

ACTIVITY 21
your lifestyle map:
navigating shared spaces

Create a basic floor plan of your home. It doesn't need to be to scale. Just be sure that each space is represented, including storage, like closets and garages, and outside spaces like decks and gardens.

You can do this exercise on your own, but it's even better to complete it with at least one other family member. Assign a color to each of four categories: 1) family spaces; 2) spaces that feel like they belong to one specific person; 3) spaces that feel comfortable and fun; 4) spaces that feel like they are off-limits. Then let each family participant have a turn marking the spaces based on how they personally feel about each area.

When everyone is finished, look over the map. Talk about what makes each space feel a given way. Maybe a room you thought of as communal has been taken over by one family member because that's where he always plays video games with his friends. Maybe another room feels uninviting because people keep bruising their shins on that darn glass coffee table. Once you have this information, decide what needs to change or be rebalanced. Jot the results in your journal.

When every member of the family is represented in the home, it can create a more vibrant, unique, and personal feeling of home.

ACTIVITY 22
personal and family values

In this exercise you will consciously inventory your family's values. Remember that every family is different (you might even be a family of one), and no one can determine your values for you. What is important is to identify what you care about, and use that as a guide as you set up your home.

In your journal make a list of your personal or family values and identify at least three objects or spaces that represent each value. As an example, I love to throw parties and want everyone to feel at ease; I never want them to feel they have to be too careful. You might say I value "comfort" and "indestructibility." Three things that represent those values in my home are: inexpensive Ikea dishes that are easily replaced, a sofa that is high quality but secondhand, and easy-to-clean wood floors.

To help get you started, I've included an example of my values list.

Rebecca's personal and family values:

Comfort   Creativity

Intelligence   Warmth

Simplicity   Independence

Affordability   Nature and time outside

Happiness   Playfulness

Travel   Cleanliness

Now it's your turn! Create your list, then—most importantly—if one or more of your values is not represented, make the changes you need to make to have that value show up in your home.

the power of play

Laughter is the best medicine, so no matter what other values you hold dear, try to make room for play. Play is serious business. It teaches us important lessons, and lets us test ideas and boundaries. Through play, we learn how to adapt and let go of expectations. The spontaneity of creative play encourages growth, keeps us young, and helps us discovers new ways of seeing the world. It's not just fun. It's essential for our survival and identity. Have you created safe space in your home for play and discovery, or is everything serious, a place where you must be careful and the rules are strictly laid out?

it's not just kid stuff

Play is just as important for adults as it is for children. Our history of play as children and the practice of play as adults make it possible to handle grown-up life. From a round of golf or game of poker to office politics and marriage, we constantly draw on the skills we learned at recess as we negotiate feelings of success, competition, and failure, and try to deal fairly and lightheartedly with others in our daily lives. Play encourages not only collaboration but also creative expression.

If we can agree that play and creativity are essential ingredients to full and meaningful lives, how do you set up a home that invites playfulness and creativity? First, make sure that there are spaces that welcome play and creativity—it's hard to explore ideas when you feel constricted by too many rules. Second, create a secure and safe environment, since neither play nor creativity can be realized when you're bound by uncertainty or fear. Third, recognize that your tastes and preferences in play and creative activities will change over time, so stay flexible. Change is natural: embrace it.

Why limit the idea of play to kid spaces? Grown ups deserve to have fun, too, and a little whimsy helps us remember not to take life too seriously.

Consider using lively color and non-traditional elements
to add personality, reduce formality, and encourage play.

live to play

How we set up our homes has everything to do with how we foster play and creativity in ourselves and in our families, but there is no one set way to accomplish this. The key is to set up the opportunity to be playful and creative, and encourage it to become a habit. At first, creativity can feel scary and uncomfortable, and it can take a while for it to come naturally. Writing that first chapter or pushing yourself out the door for that soccer game when it's cold and rainy—these habits benefit from the right environment and the right gear, especially when you are just starting a new hobby. A space that encourages you to try something new, rather than a space that defeats you before you even begin, makes successful experimentation possible.

There are no rules to what it means to be creative at home, but it is important to set aside play space that's right for you and your family. Maybe your family loves to play outdoors. You'll need a good landing zone for when all the outdoor enthusiasts come home, and accessible storage for all the fishing, camping, or sports gear. When all your gear is easy to find and ready to go when you are, you'll spend a lot less time hunting it down or tripping over it and a lot more time outdoors, where you love to be.

If you want to play more—do puzzles, practice the guitar, rebuild classic cars—you must have a space that makes it easy to settle into the activity without too much hassle. Place the puzzles out on a game table. Hang the guitar on the wall in your den. Declutter the garage so you have a place to tinker. The more you can leave the tools of the hobby out and ready to use, the more likely it is that you'll dive back in again.

Since our work-lives are often stressful, you may need a bridge from a serious day at work to a creative evening of play, so think about preparing some environmental cues. If you're a writer, prepare a desk space that looks like a writer's space. If you are an artist, leave your easel out, your paints ready to use. Set up visual cues that help shake off whatever else is on your mind and get you into a creative state, ready for art and play.

make it safe to play

If you are committed to nurturing creativity in your home, then in addition to making the tools and toys of play available, it's also important to create a home that feels safe and secure. Who can enjoy play when they feel uneasy, scrutinized, or judged? Creativity is part of self-actualization, right at the very top of Maslow's hierarchy of needs (see page 73) and you can't get to the top of the pyramid if you don't have a solid foundation meeting your family's other basic needs. Our homes should foster security, love, and acceptance, because in a secure environment, we can realize our most creative selves. Unfortunately, the places many people call home fail to meet the needs of those who live there, and that keeps the occupants from reaching their creative potential or willingly venturing out to explore the world in play.

allow for change

Finally, it's impossible to encourage play and creativity without understanding that interests will change over time. While it's important to cheer people on in their creative ventures, if we invest too emotionally in someone's current pursuit they may not feel like they have permission to change tracks and try something different. Children are probably not going to play with Lego and Barbies forever, right? Likewise, you may lose interest in knitting or woodworking, and your partner might decide he's done with golf and would rather host a monthly wine club instead. Even when you don't understand why you, your spouse, or your child has shed an interest, be assured that exploring, growing, and changing is part of the human experience and must be allowed, even encouraged. As you set up your creative home, try not to make assumptions about what can or cannot be done at a certain age. Aside from safety considerations, you can adapt nearly any activity to any age, and certainly to any gender.

With the following exercises, you'll explore changes that encourage a more creative and playful home.

Hobbies and interests change over time. As one hobby passes away, be sure to clear out unused gear so that storage space is well used and not stuffed full of neglected projects.

the curse of the incomplete craft project

Let's take an inventory of all the half-done creative projects in your house. In your journal, list any unfinished project, from quilting to candy making, computer rebuilding to vintage car restoration. Include who the project belongs to, when it was started (or, if it hasn't been started, when the supplies were purchased), and the last time someone worked on it.

Project...

Artist...

Date begun...

When complete, review your crafty to-do list. Which projects are no longer of interest? Which ones were forgotten? If discussing with others in your household, which ones can you complete as a family? Which ones can you take off the to-do list by donating the whole kit and caboodle to charity, a school, or a community center?

Remember, it's okay to say that you're no longer interested in a project. Life is too short to spend your time working on something meaningless to you and besides, someone else might be overjoyed to receive the supplies.

Please don't spend your time on something just because you spent your money on it. Money is just money, and we can make more of it, but there is nothing more precious than time. It's the one resource that is truly non-renewable.

The tools we use to pursue our passions belong in our home and should be easy to reach. The rest is clutter and needs to get out of the way (and probably out of our homes)!

ACTIVITY 24
crafty commitments

After you've finished Activity 23 with an honest assessment of all the half-done projects in the house and eliminated the craft projects you've lost interest in, it's time to consider why the other projects are not getting done. So, start a new list of the projects that you or someone else in the family wants to finish. Brainstorm and commit to changes that will help each person have creative time to finish his or her projects. Maybe you'll clear out space in the garage for model building. Maybe you'll rearrange the hall closet so supplies are readily at hand. Maybe you'll establish a weekly or monthly craft night.

Providing space where it's easy to practice your favorite creative pursuits increases the odds that you'll turn off the TV and pick up a paintbrush.

ACTIVITY 25
new adventures, old loves

This exercise gives you a chance to reflect on the ways you have changed, to let go of activities that are no longer serving you, and even return to an old project if you are so moved. In your journal, follow the guidelines below to explore how you used to play, how you play now or feel you ought to play, and how you might start to play.

WHEN I WAS A CHILD:

My favorite playtime activities were...
I had a talent for...
I was afraid to...
I always wanted to...

IN THIS CURRENT CHAPTER THAT IS NOW PASSING AWAY:

My favorite creative activities have been...
I have a talent for...
I have been afraid to...
I have been wanting to...

IN THIS NEXT CHAPTER:

I will creatively explore...
I will try my talent for...
I will have the courage to...
I will take action and...

When you have finished exploring the past, present, and future of your creative life, find one action to take toward the ideas you wrote down for your next chapter, and start making your future a reality.

work space:
set the scene for success

There are times in life when you have to make a big, bold move in your education or career. Sometimes it's a life transition, like a divorce, that demands you take on a new role. Sometimes you simply sense a calling within you, a deep and urgent need to change, learn, and grow. Regardless of what compels the shift, when it's time to learn something new, your home can be a big help in the process, or it can really get in your way.

Taking on a new career or course of study might mean that you need a quiet place to work. It might mean that you need a room where you can talk privately on the phone with clients. It might mean that you need a closet and bathroom space where you can quickly get ready each morning without waking up the rest of your household.

Whether you are an entrepreneur or an employee, work from or away-from home, your home has a profound affect on your success. How you feel when you walk in your door after work, or when you wake up and get ready in the morning, affects your self-worth and how you expect people to relate to you in your professional world. When you look around your home, do you see the home of a self-assured, confident person in charge of her destiny and success? Or is your home, and are you, controlled by circumstances that feel out of your influence? How would you feel if a coworker or your boss were to drop by your home unannounced?

At its best, the space of a professional, career-minded person feels focused, successful, even powerful. It's a space that changes the behavior of both the professional person who works there and the clients and workers who enter it.

A home office that reflects and reinforces a sense of self-assurance makes us feel great about our work and our success in life.

If you are contemplating growing into a new professional role, consider creating a space that already looks like the success you plan to achieve. If you start each day by walking into the office of a successful, career-minded woman, you are much more likely to conduct yourself like a successful woman, and the world will respond to you that way. You will be your own self-fulfilling prophecy. But it works in reverse, too. If every day you walk into an office that looks like it's occupied by a lazy, disorganized, discouraged worker, you will see yourself that way, and the universe will treat you as such.

You've heard the expression "Dress for the job you want." The same logic applies to the home office. Creating a successful space doesn't mean you have to invest in a $10,000 mahogany desk. Successful doesn't equal expensive. But it does mean you should be living and working in a space that feels future-focused and successful to you. How we dress our home can have as great an impact on our upward mobility as how we dress ourselves.

the environment of the entrepreneur

Improving your office can have nearly magical power, one that surprises even those of us who work in the field of design. My colleague Stacy made over her own home office and, without any other changes, saw a fifty percent increase in her business. Was that because her new space allowed her to concentrate better? Was it because she exuded renewed strength and success, and her clients responded to that new energy? Probably both. Whatever the reason, it's not a very big risk to change our space, and the potential rewards are huge.

Choose design elements for your home and workspace that inspire you and help you focus on what you are working toward.

cluttered desk, cluttered mind?

When I'm asked, "Does a cluttered desk matter?" I notice that whoever is asking usually has a bias. Messy people ask with the hope that they don't have to go home and tidy up, and tidy people ask it with an air of knowingness, just certain that I'll back up their assertion that cleanliness is next to godliness. I don't think there is one right answer. We all have different sensitivities to clutter, and our job is to figure out our own tolerance for clutter and, of course, balance that with the impression of stability and professionalism we want to give our clients.

Studies show that the "right" amount of clutter can boost your creativity, while the "wrong" amount of clutter can elevate your stress. And stress not only hurts your creativity in the short term, it hurts your health in the long term. But what is the "right" amount of clutter? That depends on your job, your team, and your personal tolerance. Just try to be honest with yourself. Is your clutter getting in the way of your success, making it hard to focus, a challenge to find what you need, and creating an unprofessional environment? If that messy desk works for you, who am I to ask you to change it? But if that same messy desk is actually a source of confusion, frustration, embarrassment, or procrastination, then of course you should change it.

client considerations: when people are going to visit your space

What if you do have clients come to your office? Whether you work from, or away from, your home, the importance of your space just jumped to a whole new level. Whether you like it or not, potential clients will assess you by your office just like they do your clothes, voice, hygiene, and smile. I remember walking into an office when I was looking for a new accountant and being greeted by forests of paper piled precariously, fields of empty coffee cups, and grimy walls with a single too-small print hanging askew behind the desk. That person may have been the world's most brilliant accountant, but the space suggested that she was overwhelmed by her work and made me question whether deadlines would be met and details addressed. Is that fair? It doesn't matter if it's fair. We judge people by how they look and what they surround themselves with,

Even when we are the only people who will ever see our workspace, the effect our workspace has on us influences our success and professionalism.

so be intentional with your space. And if you don't have the time or talent to create a professional work environment for yourself, hire it out. Once you understand that your space has an emotional and economic impact on the success of your company, it becomes clear that hiring a pro isn't foolish: it's a brilliant use of your time and money.

safety first

If you are inviting clients into your home, you absolutely must create a space that feels professional and safe. We know that first impressions are essential, and a bad first impression may be your only impression. As you decide where to have your office, look at it from two perspectives: yours and your clients'.

Case in point: I consulted with a life coach who was setting up a home office. Since the top level of his three-story town home had the best light and a nice layout, he thought that would make a great workspace. During our consultation I asked him whether he anticipated having female clients (yes) and then pointed out the obvious: female clients might not feel all that comfortable traipsing through a single guy's private home, up three levels, to the farthest point from the front door. I suggested he use the lowest-level room for his office—it not only had a bathroom nearby but was also located right next to the front door and had French doors that opened onto a back patio. This change created an experience that was more professional and more comfortable for the client.

When planning your office space, think about the impression it will make on your clients and any anxieties clients may be bringing into a meeting. Consider the location of the space in your home relative to safety (both yours and the client's), to distractions from family members and pets, and to comfort. Also consider the geography of your home and neighborhood: How will clients enter the home? Where will they park? Many small businesses are run from the home, but the most successful small businesses put a lot of thought and intention behind the space itself and the client experience.

The "right" amount of clutter inspires creativity. The "wrong" amount elevates stress. Only you know the balance that is just right for your success.

If clients visit your home office, your design choices will not only influence their confidence in you professionally, but also affect how comfortable and safe they feel in your space.

what if clients never see your space?

Many entrepreneurs and freelancers work from home and no one else ever sees their workspace. Does it really matter what it looks like? Absolutely! Let's take, for instance, your office chair. If it is uncomfortable, shabby, and doesn't promote good posture, your clients will hear that when you speak with them on the phone. What? Really? Yes! Try recording your voicemail message in two ways. First, record the message sitting slouched on a squishy chair, and don't smile. Listen to the recording and note the energy in your voice. Then record the same message sitting or even standing with excellent posture, and smile. Listen to the alternative—you might be surprised by how much more alive, capable, and happy the second message sounds.

Take some simple steps to boost the mood in your workspace. Be sure the furniture helps you sit comfortably and properly. Modify the layout so you can easily access what you need. Freshen up the design to make you feel happy and successful so that clients can hear the smile in your voice. Surround yourself with things that help you work well and feel great, and remind you of what you are working towards.

Refresh your workspace regularly, perhaps every six months or so. That doesn't mean you have to completely redecorate, but at least take down the holiday cards, put up current family pictures, and clean away all the dust behind your computer. Over time we stop seeing whatever is right in front of our eyes, but that doesn't mean it doesn't send an unconscious message to our minds. Make sure your space helps you feel energetic and successful, not shabby and obsolete.

ready, set, launch

If you have career advancement in mind and picture a bright future for yourself, then do what it takes to set yourself up for success. It's important to take action toward the new venture. If you just say you are committed to a new path but you are reluctant to let go of old habits, then the universe is going to let you keep the old ways. It will respond to your actions, not your words.

If you really want to propel forward, allow the old you to make way for the new you. It's hard to stride ahead confidently while you're carrying a bunch of old baggage. You need those hands free to grab opportunities! Does that mean you have to throw everything out and start over? Of course not. But you benefit by taking an honest look

Taking time out from working on your business to improve on your workspace may feel unimportant, but pays dividends in focus, efficiency, and self-confidence, all of which can lead to greater financial success.

at your life, your home, and your office, and taking stock of the messages you are sending yourself.

As you set the scene for a new level of success, connect with the reason why you are going to make some changes, and keep that front and center as you change your space. This will help you figure out if your space just needs organizing and a fresh coat of paint, whether it needs new furniture and some built-in storage, or if it is time to invest in an office away from home. Without that clarity, you may not end up with the results you need, and risk wasting your time and money.

The exercises that follow should help create clarity around your why and give you some tools for success, too.

ACTIVITY 26
setting the scene for success

What does success look and feel like for you? In your journal explore the following questions to identify where your existing space might not be meeting your needs so you can create positive changes.

1. Write down your career or education goal...

2. Identify a mentor or role model in that field...

3. Use your imagination to think of what your mentor's or role model's workspace might look like. What kind of chair might they have? Desk? What books line their shelves?

4. Now look at your workspace and, as if you did not work there, describe the person who works there. Based only on what you see, what do they do? What are their strengths, and what are their weaknesses? Judge as objectively as you can. Is this someone you would trust with your money? Is this the office of a successful person in your field?

5. Based on your answers to the above, and the alignment between how you imagine your mentor might work and live and how you are currently working and living, create an action list of three powerful changes you could make to your space, and the differences these changes will make.

After you identify three actions, mark on your calendar dates by which you will accomplish each action and how you will get it done. By each action, note resources you'll need to get it done.

ACTIVITY 27
now and later

In this activity, let's look at where you are emotionally and physically in your work life at present and where you would like to be in the future. In your journal complete each phrase below with descriptive words that fit how you feel now, and how you wish to feel later.

at work now:	at work later:
I feel...	I will feel...
It feels...	It will feel...
My chair is...	My chair will be...
Starting a project feels...	Starting a project will feel...
Finishing a project feels...	Finishing a project will feel...
The place where I take a break is...	The place where I take a break will be...
When I answer a phone call I...	When I answer a phone call I will...
When I get stuck I...	When I get stuck I will...
My computer is...	My computer will be...
I share my space with...	I will share my space with...
I wish I could...	I will be able to...
When I reach for something I need it is...	When I reach for something I need it will be...

Read your answers and note three important discrepancies between your at-work now and at-work later descriptions.

Now, most importantly, identify how things will change after you modify the space. Take a few minutes and imagine how you will feel, what you will accomplish, and what success will feel like when you are working in a space that supports you. Really feel it, taste it, touch it, listen to it. What does the floor feel like under your feet? What scents fill the air? What snacks are on hand to nourish you? What colors surround you? (NOTE: For a guide to visualizing your new workspace, visit www.happystartsathome.com and try "Put the Om in Your Home," a twenty-minute guided meditation.) After your reflection in your journal complete the following sentence:

After I commit to changing my workspace, I will...

We spend at least a quarter of our adult life at work, so why
not do it in a space that makes you feel hopeful about the
future and helps you be the professional you want to be?

spirituality:
care for your soul connection

What does it mean to have a spiritual home? Is it a home where you meditate daily? A home with corner shrines? A home that hosts Bible studies? It could be any of these things and still not actually be a spiritual home. It could be none of these things and yet be a deeply spiritual home. If there is no one way to create a spiritual home, how do you make sure that your home is meeting your spiritual needs? As you've done with all of the other slices of life, identify what spirituality means to you, how you need to be supported in your faith, and what needs to change in your home to do that.

Sometimes our spiritual lives seem to be experienced only at a retreat or in a house of worship. I have experienced spiritual renewal everywhere from my childhood church in suburban Michigan to a silent meditation retreat in the middle of a Pacific Northwest rainforest. Each time, though, my connection to spirit seems to fade as I reenter "real life" and face the chaos of balancing the work, housekeeping, and relationships in my life. Can you relate to that struggle? Let's invite spirituality into our homes.

Small and simple design choices, such as a treasured spiritual artwork or symbol, can connect our home to our faith, and keep us quietly focused on what matters even as we go about the activities of daily life.

bringing spirituality home

How can you bring the meditation retreat home? How can you make sure that your spiritual needs are met in your home so that you are constantly in touch with what deeply matters to you? If we accept that your spirituality is an essential thread in the fabric of your life, then naturally we need to make sure it is represented in your home and that your faith is supported and nurtured. Spirituality at home has three components: what you have, what you do not have, and what you do.

what do you have in your home?

Creating a spiritual home is less about things and more about space—to breathe. To be. To meditate. To pray. Do you have space in your home where you can practice your faith?

For some people, a spiritual home means literally having an altar or meditation space. It can help clear the mind and literally create space for worship or reflection. Research shows that as little as three minutes a day of meditation has great power, so why not create a space that helps you focus? Something as small as a smooth rock, or as large as a whole guest room turned into a meditation space, can support you in resting your mind and letting things flow again. My client Monica had a lovely, airy, rarely used guest bedroom. What she really needed was a space where, after a long, hectic day in her medical practice, she could quiet her mind and reconnect with the meaningful things in her life. We made over the room with a lovely daybed so it could double as a guest and meditation room. Of course we can't always closet ourselves away when we need to get in touch with our faith. That means that a spiritual home won't just have special spaces for prayer and meditation—it will also allow you to connect with what is meaningful while doing even the most mundane stuff like cleaning the cat box or making the bed.

As you think about your home, perhaps you want to set up a specific meditation or prayer space, but consider the big picture of your home too. It's possible to create harmony between your spiritual needs and your living spaces. Make sure that what you value is seen and reflected as you look around your home. Many of my Christian clients display beautiful crosses. Many of my Buddhist clients have altars. One symbol of your faith, however, can't counter a house full of items that show a contradictory set of values. If you say that your deepest values center on nature but your home is overfilled

As you look around your home, do you feel it accurately represents the values you hold dear? Could someone else come over and get a sense of what matters to you just by being in your home?

with low-quality, rarely used stuff, does that align with your values? If you say that your deepest values center on family and connection with others, but your whole home is focused on TV and screen time, does that align with your values? If your God is a god of loving kindness, simplicity, and generosity, do you see that in your home? If you connect to Spirit by being surrounded by friends and family, it is essential to set up a home that makes it easy to gather and entices people to linger. If you connect to Spirit by retreating into silence and prayer, set aside a private, sacred spot. And if you connect by surrounding yourself with nature, make sure you have easy access to the outdoors.

what should leave your home?

Creating a spiritual home is as much about what you do not have as it is about what you do have. Perhaps more so. Our lives are, quite frankly, overstimulating. There is too much noise, too many options, too much input for us to hear the voice of our conscience, of our instincts, or of God or Spirit. The only way we know to cope is to tune out and turn off. We know we pay a price in the quantity and quality of our experiences and miss opportunities to connect socially, but with such relentless stimulation attacking us, it's as if we have no choice. We shut down just so we don't implode. We tune out in response to the overstimulation of our outside environments, yet then we turn around and compound that with overstimulation at home. Junk mail, kids' toys, television, radio, newspapers, cell phones, email . . . It's no wonder we can't hear our own inner voice or the voice of the universe. We must create space for silence, for retreat, and for calm. What better place to do that than in the place you call home?

That means we probably have to let go of a bunch of stuff. We have to stop hoarding. And hoarding may not look quite like what you imagine. Hoarders are not just those poor souls on TV who are barricaded inside their own homes with decades of trash or two-for-one purchases. Hoarding is found in every ungenerous choice we make. It shows up every time we stuff yet another lidless piece of Tupperware in the already-crowded cabinet. It is found when we refuse to create space for our partner's preferences. Every time we are ungenerous we are lacking in faith, because faith permits us to let go and know that we have and will have everything we need.

Creating a spiritual home means letting go of the stories we tell ourselves, like "I don't have enough." "I am always broke." "I don't know what's going to come; better to be safe than sorry." Out of fear we hold tightly to our narratives. Why hold on to something now just in case you need it, when you can give it to someone who needs it and to whom it will bring joy now? Why not have enough faith to be generous today, and trust that the universe will provide for you tomorrow? It is so easy to live in a state of fear. Our culture, especially the media, bombards us with Buy now! Act now! Don't miss this show tonight! What we see, we believe. Try turning down the volume on all those messages (maybe by turning off the screens in your home?) and listening for the voice of God or Spirit in your home and in your life.

A spiritual home leaves room—physically and emotionally—for reflection, quiet, and connection.

what do you do in your home?

Your home is the foundation of everything in your life—including your faith.

Compare the tenets of your faith to the behavior going on in your home and in your heart. Do you wish to practice forgiveness, but find yourself wallowing in anger at your ex instead of letting the past be the past? Look around. If reminders of your past relationship surround you and keep you tied to old hurts, you will find it hard to let go. It's hard enough to release past injuries, but so much harder to practice forgiveness if you are surrounded by pain. But if you create a space that allows you to move on, you'll find that you can more easily practice forgiveness because you are able to look forward instead of backward. Many of us hold tightly to our past in large part because it feels good to have that past to blame. But if you want to fully align with your spiritual self, you'd do well to let go visually, physically, and emotionally.

Do you wish to practice kindness and consideration? Take a look at the activities and games in your home. Are they all screen-focused or solo-play games? Consider making your main areas screen-free and choosing games that encourage teamwork and sharing. By having to interact and to negotiate, we learn to accommodate other people's needs and to practice being considerate. What we play, we learn, and it influences our behavior outside the home.

Do you wish to practice generosity? Look at your belongings and consider how much comes in versus how much goes out. A simple one-in, one-out rule can help you balance giving and receiving. It can apply to shoes, games, coats, even relationships and money. To fully commit yourself to a new partner, it is important to release the baggage of old relationships and let the new relationship grow on its own foundation. And when it comes to money, the simple principle of tithing reminds you that 10 percent of what you receive is meant to be given back.

Do you wish to practice gratitude? Gratitude is a central tenet of prayer, especially before meals. If your busy home and lifestyle prevent your family from gathering around the table to celebrate a meal and show gratitude for the bounty, a change might be in order.

These small, incremental changes are like drops in a bucket, and over time, you'll find your bucket full. Just celebrating your faith and values as a family one more time a week than before means you are growing in alignment with your faith. In time it will come more naturally and you will come to crave that time with the calm and support of the universe.

If connecting with your family or your faith over a meal is important to you, create a dedicated, distraction-free dining space, and put it to use as often as you can.

leave room for spiritual growth

Setting up a spiritual home isn't a one-time event. Spiritual homes are not stagnant. That is because what you need from your home, and in your home, will change over time. The systems that worked for you five years ago might not work for you now. How has your life changed in the last decade? New job? New family? New hobbies? New friends? Unexpected health challenges? As input and demands shift, you'll want to adjust your home to meet your new needs. Finally, the spiritual home reminds us that in the end we own nothing. Our connection to the otherworldly has nothing to do with our sofas, cars, or TVs.

The key to happiness lies in appreciating the little things—cherish and display the things that matter to you.

A spiritual home may be minimalist or maximalist. The key isn't about the quantity of things in the house, but rather that abundance is intentional, only including things and activities that align with the values of those who live there.

ACTIVITY 28
love letters

Even with its flaws, a home is a blessing. For the next thirty days, keep a journal of love letters to your home. Recognize and appreciate what you have, rather than focus on the long list of everything that needs to get done. Write at least one full page of gratitudes, large and small, for the things in your home. Here are journal examples:

Thank you for hot showers. Thank you for a roof over my head. Thank you for east-facing windows that let in morning light. Thank you for a room for each of my kids. Thank you for flushing toilets. Thank you for a dishwasher . . .

If you have been practicing negativity lately, you may find this exercise surprisingly hard at first, but stay with it. Yes, frustrations exist, but for five minutes of the morning, choose to ignore those frustrations while you write the love letter to your home.

There is no magic to the words—the magic is in the practice. Focus on what you have rather than what you do not have. Is there anything more spiritual?

ACTIVITY 29
eliminating distractions

This one is a toughy. Are you actually committed to having a spiritual home? It may be time to unplug (gasp!). You are in control here, and only you know the biggest distractions that keep you from having open communication with God or Spirit. For me, busyness is one big distraction. TV is another. The radio in the car is a third. And food is a fourth.

Think through your day and identify the top three distractions that keep you from having more conversations with God or Spirit. The things you do in moments of weakness to feel better, when perhaps it would have been better to draw directly from the Well. Identify your top three distractions and pick one of the three and commit to a day, a week, or a month without that distraction. You are in charge here, and only you can identify the achievable challenge that is right for you. When you are halfway through the period of eliminating distraction #1, add distraction #2. When you are halfway through the period of eliminating distraction #2, add distraction #3. Try to do the morning writing exercise (Activity 28, Love Letters) in tandem with this exercise. The love letters will help you keep your commitment to clearing distractions and listening for your soul's care and connection throughout the day.

Create space in your home for daily rituals that are free
from distractions, and use those spaces to develop habits
that help you become your best self.

self-worth:
say yes to a happy home

The colors we choose, the objects and books we place on our shelves, the pictures and posters we put on the walls—we select them because of what they add to our lives and homes, both functionally and esthetically. But the items and elements are also projections, or "messages" from the unconscious, the same way that our dreams contain such messages. What messages are we letting our home send us every morning when we wake up and every evening as we go to sleep? This chapter is about boundaries. Creating healthy boundaries around whom and what we let into our lives, and to which voices we are willing to listen. It's about ignoring (or embracing) trends, and permitting change over time. The walls and mirrors of your home reflect your self-worth and self-image and send an inescapable message about what you feel you deserve and your place in this world.

A happy home puts a smile on your face the moment you walk in the door.

look, listen, and shine a light

A home that reflects a high level of self-worth is not necessarily one filled with expensive, fancy furnishings. Likewise, a home filled with secondhand furniture and Craigslist finds doesn't necessarily reflect a low self-image. I have found no correlation between cost of furnishings and happiness. I have noticed other correlations, however.

Indications of low self-worth:
• Too many belongings

• Dust on all the belongings

• Lack of pictures or art

• Broken things

• Unpacked boxes

• Inherited paint colors, especially from ex-partners

• Dirty walls

• Museum-perfect spaces

• Offices that have become storage rooms

• Naked bedrooms

• All rooms overrun with kid toys

• Dangerous furniture (like glass-cornered coffee tables)

As you examine how your home reflects your self-worth, your home's entry is a wonderful place to start. Let's try this: I'll describe two of my clients' entries, both their public and their for-family-use-only doorways, and you think about how you'd feel approaching each entry. At the first client's main entry, you approach a freshly painted high-gloss yellow door flanked by flowerpots brimming with freshly watered flowers. The sconce by the door is free of cobwebs, and the light comes on brightly as you approach at dusk. The house numbers are large and easy to read, and the welcome mat is freshly swept. The family tends to use a second entrance that goes through the garage and straight into the laundry room, where the floors are scrubbed and the walls are freshly painted. A recently vacuumed doormat inside the garage door catches extra dirt,

We take better care of ourselves in spaces that reflect success and confidence.

and a series of cubbies capture shoes and coats. Recycle bins are handy so that junk mail never makes it into the house, and this year's calendar smiles brightly from the wall.

At the second client's main entry, the door paint is peeling, the door panels are crusted with grime, and a faded holiday wreath greets visitors even though it's early summer. The plants in the neglected pot are long dead from lack of water. The house numbers are small and closely match the color of the house, making them hard to read. This home also has a second door that the family enters through the garage into the laundry room, where the dirty vinyl floor is covered in mismatched shoes, and dust bunnies mix with lost socks by the dryer. The walls haven't been painted since the house was built, so the door frames are covered in greasy handprints, as is the paint around the light switches and door handle. A three-year-old calendar is thumbtacked to the wall, and a pile of junk mail perches precariously on top of the washer next to the laundry pile.

Beyond the superficial visual differences, the more important distinction between these entries is in how they make you feel as you enter. Every single day you'd either walk into a home that greets you with a smile and reminds you that your hard work has paid off, or into a home that meets you with a frown and makes you wonder why you bother. The care and setup of your house says either "welcome home" or "I give up" (or even "go away").

The entry to your home can't help but send you a daily message. A cluttered coat rack may imply that you have no boundaries and no ability to filter what is allowed into your life. A pile of stuff you meant to donate months ago may suggest that you can't commit to letting go. Certainly you deserve a better "welcome home!"

seeing your home with new eyes

Living amid clutter doesn't mean you are afraid of letting go and facing truth, but it can mean that. Hanging art won't necessarily flood your life with instant positivity, but it can do that. The process of looking at our homes as mirrors of ourselves is a tool to use as part of an honest evaluation. Our choices—in words, clothes, friends—all the things we surround ourselves with, and the way we treat ourselves and allow ourselves to be treated, signal what is going on inside our minds. Because we react to, and mirror, our surroundings, changing them will, by design, help us change ourselves. Open up to change by altering the environments in which you work, live, love, and play.

What does your entry say about you? How does it make you feel?

We have to treat ourselves the way we wish to be treated by others, and that includes living in a situation that is healthful and supportive. When we let things fall apart around us, and accommodate things that are shabby, broken, and dangerous instead of demanding better for ourselves, we send out a message to the universe that we are not worthy, that we do not deserve anything better than what we have. Those messages are reinforced every day when we struggle against a closet door that won't slide open easily, or we look into a broken mirror each morning, or we use pliers to press the lever on the toaster because the handle broke off months ago. If your friend could afford a new toaster and yet you saw how she struggled with the broken one every morning, you would probably encourage her to get rid of that frustrating old appliance. Don't you deserve the same consideration? It can start by changing out something as simple as one burnt-out lightbulb. Shine a light on a new, improved life.

the good, the bad, and the familiar

Why do we let ourselves remain stuck in frustrating situations and unpleasant spaces for so long? The reason is simple: we cling to our habits because they do something for us, they serve a purpose. We keep conditions around us static because they are familiar, comfortable. To behave in a new way, the need for something new must outweigh the need for what we have now. Oftentimes, even though we say we want something new, it's more that we think we should want something new. In reality we'd rather stick with what we know.

Clutter can be comforting if it keeps you from having to face the truth (like sorting through the stuff from your childhood or addressing all the disappointing purchases you've made). For some people, a messy house protects them because it means they don't have to engage socially. (What better excuse not to have someone over than if the house isn't "ready"?) A closed-off entry prevents you from inviting anyone in. An unusable kitchen excuses an unhealthy lifestyle. An office-turned-storage room stops you from launching a freelance business. A TV-focused living room frees you from facing uncomfortable conversations within the family. A kid-overrun bedroom excuses the lack of intimacy in your marriage.

If you are ready for a more honest life, it will mean changing habits. It will mean changing what is around you. At first it may be deeply uncomfortable.

Your home should help you have, not hold you back from, your best life, so if it ever gets in the way of having people over, makes you feel embarrassed, or keeps you from getting important things done, change it!

color yourself into a new state of happiness

Changing your self-image is the hardest work of all, because the voices in your head are often the loudest, and no one else can hear them and tell them to be quiet for you. That is why the home can be such a powerful tool for transforming your idea of self-worth. Instead of beating your head against the proverbial wall and trying to change your thoughts, try focusing your energy on changing the paint color on your walls. Having been there myself, I can tell you that a remarkable transformation can happen in your heart as you watch the walls go from one color to another. Later, as you scrub the paint out of your hair and out from under your fingernails, you'll find yourself uncovering not just a new room, but a new you.

Little actions start the gears moving on a beautiful cycle of renewal. Hang a fresh pair of drapes. Scrub the tile so it gleams. Rid the closet of all your ill-fitting clothes. Replace all the burnt-out lightbulbs. I guarantee you'll start to feel better. You'll hold your head a little higher. You'll smile just a little more easily. Then someone will smile back. And you'll have started a chain reaction that can lead to more positivity, and help not only yourself but also everyone you touch. That's about as selfless as it gets.

Don't be afraid to take a risk with your paint color. It's a great way to practice courage and prepares you for being bold out in the real world.

our homes, ourselves

Can I tell you some of the things I love about my home? In my bathroom I have light sconces on either side of the mirror so that the light never accentuates bags under my eyes. The walls of my bedroom are painted deep navy blue, and I have blackout drapes over my windows so that I can easily close out the world and get a really deep night of sleep. In my living room I have several adorable creatures: an owl pillow, a stuffed leather frog, and the coolest unicorn skull made by a local potter.

Why do each of these things matter? Because they help me feel happier at home. When I remodeled my master bath I installed warm side-lighting instead of harsh overhead-lighting because I don't need bathroom lighting that adds ten years to my face. (You know how horrible you feel after looking at your body in a bad dressing room under fluorescent lights? Bad bathroom lighting does that to you daily.) I chose deep, sensual, rich colors for the walls and light-controlling curtains for my bedroom so that it's me, not the neighborhood streetlights, that controls my go-to-sleep experience. When I get a good night of sleep, my world is a better place. I have more energy, more joy, and much more patience! And the creatures in my living room? They simply make me smile!

a room of your own

Even in childhood we build pillow forts and cardboard box homes and try to control who may come in and who may not. We all need a private spot where we can be alone. Long after we stop creating our fantasy play spaces, we still have a need for a room (or at least a corner) where we imagine no one can find us. Where we can be left in peace. Many of us fondly remember our first apartment. Why, despite the cockroaches, the broken lock, and the creepy guy down the hall, does it always have a special golden glow in our memory? Because it was the first time we got to be king or queen of the castle, featherer of our own nest. In our childhood home decisions were out of our hands and our rooms were never really ours to control. But in our first place, there is no one but us to determine how we shall live, when we will come home, what the walls will say about this new, unbounded, free-to-fly adult called "you."

There is something special about knowing a space belongs to just you. It can make the rest of the world just a little easier to handle.

say yes to new adventures

We know children need to express their emerging identities, separate from parents or siblings, through the personalization of space. But of course growth, change, and development doesn't stop with childhood. It continues on as we land our first job, partner with a lover, raise children, send the kids away from home, retire. With each transition we need to continually express our emerging identities. If your house stays stuck for two decades, your spirit does too. If you choose not to make changes, are you afraid of losing what you had, fearful that nothing better will come along? That you will lose your youth? Is it possible that you're afraid the best days of your life have passed by? There must be a balance between holding on and letting go, and you must develop faith that you are wonderful enough to have another amazing chapter of your life story. It can be scary to let go of who you were, or who you once believed yourself to be. It can be a lot less scary to play with the edges of those possibilities by changing your environment. The very ordinariness of new sheets or new posters on the walls is exactly what makes them so powerful. By making those little changes you can slowly, step by step, walk out of your old life and into a new one.

Let your home develop, change and unfold over time—it will create space for you to do the same.

ACTIVITY 30
old baggage: assumptions, power, procrastination, denial, and fear

In this exercise we'll explore what may be holding you back from change. As you read through this list of statements I have heard from clients, note in your journal any that resonate with you:

beliefs and assumptions: what excuses are you hiding behind?

- Trying to declutter won't do any good; my husband won't let go of anything.
- I've failed before; it'll just get bad again.
- I'm not good at decorating; I have no taste.
- I have to keep this because my sister/mom/friend/mother-in-law gave it to me.
- I have to keep this because it was my grandmother's/daughter's.
- My partner doesn't see the need for change, and so he won't let me make changes.
- This clutter isn't really affecting my family/relationships/health/work.
- If I make changes, my mom/husband/kids won't understand.
- Whatever I do, it won't be enough.
- Whatever I do, it needs to be perfect.
- It's not right to get rid of these things.
- I might need these things some day.
- "They" might need these things some day.
- It's selfish to focus on creating space for me.
- It's selfish to create a beautiful home when a lot of people don't even have a home.
- It's too much work; it's too expensive; it will take too long.
- I'm just not an organized person.

If your best friend were to say these things to you, what advice would you give them?

power struggles: who or what are you allowing to have power over you?

- I'm waiting for the right time.
- This isn't my forever home.
- I don't own this home.
- I moved into my new partner's home, and I can't change anything.
- I don't have the right coach/book/class/tools.
- My home is too small.
- My home is too big.
- I am not healthy enough.
- I am too tired.
- I can't get time off work.
- It's not my stuff.
- It's just part of having kids.
- It's just part of being married.
- They have to change first.
- As soon as I get... then I'll do it.
- I don't want to hurt them.
- Only rich people live in nice homes.

If your best friend were giving up this kind of control over their own life, what advice would you give them?

procrastination: how are you excusing your delay?

- I'll do it later.
- I can't think right now.
- I don't have time right now.
- It would take too much time away from my work/parenting.
- I have too many other things to do.
- I'll do it as soon as I get through with...
- I'll do it as soon as I get back from...
- The time isn't right; it's too late/it's too soon.

If your best friend were making these excuses, what advice would you give them?

denial: is your head in the sand?

- There isn't a problem.
- It's not my problem.
- I can't do anything about this problem.
- Changing things wouldn't do any good.
- The problem will go away if I ignore it.

If your best friend were hiding from the truth, what advice would you give them?

fear: what are you hiding from?

- I'm not ready yet.
- I might fail.
- They might reject me.
- What will they think?
- I'm afraid to tell my spouse things are not working.
- I might get hurt.
- I may have to change.
- It might cost money.
- I would rather get a divorce first.
- I don't want anyone to know I have a problem.
- I don't want to talk about it.
- I don't have the energy.
- It's too hard.
- I wouldn't be perfect.
- I might lose my friends.
- It might hurt my image.
- I'm not good enough.

If your best friend shared these fears with you, what advice would you give them?

Sometimes we need to look at our homes—and our lives—with fresh eyes and ask: what do I know that is true, and what could actually be different?

ACTIVITY 31
questions to identify and defeat limiting beliefs

Choose three to six statements from Activity 30, the ones that really struck a chord in your heart. List them in your journal. For example, you might have resonated with:

- I might fail.
- Changing things wouldn't do any good.
- I don't have time right now.

- The problem will go away if I ignore it.
- My home is too small.
- It's selfish to focus on creating space for me.

Coaches who focus on identifying and eliminating these kinds of internalized beliefs like to challenge their clients with this simple question: "Is this really true?" Just because you believe it doesn't necessarily make it true. Now let's explore how you will defeat your limiting beliefs.

Look at the statements you have chosen from Activity 30 and answer the following questions:

- Are they true? Are they really true?
  What would happen if they were not true?
- What dream are these thoughts preventing me from realizing?
  How are these pessimistic thoughts protecting me?
- Who in my family used to (or still does) makes similar statements?
  How do I feel when I hear this from other people?
- Are these beliefs keeping me from obtaining what I want?
  Does that feel safe?
- Do I value something that contradicts what I say I want for my home and my life?
- What "failures" in my past have "proven" these statements?
  Am I allowing these so-called failures to keep me from trying something new?
- What black-and-white philosophies do these statements reveal that keep me frozen in a passive way?

Review your answers and decide if that is how you wish to live the rest of your life story. You can't rewrite the past, but you sure do have control over the next chapter. You are the author of your own story, and you can write the words of power and positivity on the walls of your very own home!

Your home can be your best friend. Make sure it's showing up for you.

conclusion

Our outer reality is a reflection of our inner reality, and we can shift our inner reality by making changes to our outer reality. When your life is congruent, meaning that your walk and your talk—or your prayers and your actions—are in alignment, you can be whole and complete. If you are not walking your talk, awareness of that dissonance is the first key to change. Once you have committed to change, the next step is to gather the tools you need to create change. Your home can be one of the easiest and most powerful tools in your journey toward a new way of living. If you have worked through the exercises in this book, you have developed that awareness. That is fantastic!

Now that you've started to see your home with new eyes, the key is to take action. But not just any action—inspired action. Have intention behind your work. Action without intent is just busy work and won't necessarily get you where you want to go. But identify what you want in your life, whether it is new love, more wealth, better family dynamics, improved health, or a livelier social life, and take action to support that intent, and you will open the channel for the universe to bring goodness into your life.

the not-so-secret keys to success

When I work with clients who are ready to create a home that really and truly supports their life, we use many of the same tools you'll find in any how-to book on organizing, decorating, and designing. It's a lot like dieting: the basic rules never change, and there are no secrets that only designers know. It's just a matter of applying the guidelines around proportions, textures, contrast, etc., in a way that creates a pleasing space, just as losing weight is technically just a matter of planning low-calorie, high-nutrition meals and making exercise a regular habit.

Of course we all know that losing weight isn't quite that easy, and keeping the weight off long term works only when you understand why you are losing weight, who you are losing weight for, and what you will gain from all that effort. Going on a diet without that strong foundation generally leads to disappointment, but going on a diet with that strong foundation can inspire a brand new lifestyle and lead to long-term, healthy change.

The same goes for feeling dissatisfied with your home's appearance. If you update based only on the latest trends, you are missing the step that ensures you will end up creating a home that is not only pleasing to the eye but also nurturing to the soul.

The key is to start with the why. Ask yourself, "Why do I need to make a change to this space?" Consider your final destination. How do you want your life to be different after you invest your time and money in your home? Will it pay off in an emotional and a supportive way? Before you lift a paintbrush, take time to figure out what you want to add to, and eliminate from, your home and your life. Clean, organize, and remodel your home with a focus on what you want to invite into your life. By letting your goals guide every action and every choice, you'll connect your home to the bigger picture of how you want to live. This way, you'll never waste energy on useless action, and you'll find yourself rewarded for your efforts by achieving your bigger goals.

Remember, it's not about what would make a "happy home" for someone else—it's just about what it means for you, and for the people with whom you share your space.

Remember, just as you should never stop exploring, learning, and growing, your home will never be "done." That means it's not a race, and you don't have to do it all at once, or perfectly. You can't. The point is simply to figure out something you need from your home, and take some small action toward that goal.

And please know that you do not have to go it alone. It is okay to seek the help of professional organizers, decorators, and contractors. Just be sure that you've set your intentions first and that your helpers are eager and excited to focus on that goal, and not a goal of their own.

home is the heart of your happiness

Life is filled with challenges, and it takes courage to do what needs to be done and change what needs to change. Sometimes, instead of taking the challenge head on— asking your boss for a raise, eliminating sugar from your diet, finding a life partner —you can first shift things in your home to create an environment that will support the new goal. This small act can give you the courage for the bigger challenge, and send a message to the universe that you are ready to receive that new money, new body, and new love.

I hope that by reading this book you see new ways in which your life could be working better and your home can support you. After all, the purpose of having a house is to live your life out of it.

May your home always be happy.

selected bibliography

Arnold, Jeanne E., Anthony P. Graesch, Enzo Ragazzini, and Elinor Ochs. *Life at Home in the Twenty-first Century: 32 Families Open Their Doors.* 1st ed. Los Angeles: Cotsen Institute of Archaeology Press, 2012.

Byrne, Rhonda. *The Secret.* New York: Atria Books/Beyond Words, 2006.

Chiazzari, Suzy. *Our Place: Improve Your Home, Improve Your Relationship.* New York: Watson-Guptill, 2002.

Csikszentmihalyi, Mihaly. *Flow: The Psychology of Optimal Experience.* 1st ed. New York: Harper Perennial, 1990.

Gallagher, Winifred. *House Thinking: A Room-by-Room Look at How We Live.* New York: HarperCollins, 2006.

Gallagher, Winifred. *The Power of Place: How Our Surroundings Shape Our Thoughts, Emotions, and Actions.* New York: HarperPerennial, 1994.

Gillingham-Ryan, Maxwell. *Apartment Therapy: The Eight-Step Home Cure.* New York: Bantam Dell, 2006.

Goode, Randa. "A Little Messiness Never Hurt Anyone," March 10, 2014, http://www.randagoode.com/a-little-messiness-never-hurt-anyone/

Hay, Louise. *You Can Heal Your Life.* Carlsbad, CA: Hay House, 1984.

Jameson, Marni. *The House Always Wins: Create the Home You Love—Without Busting Your Budget.* Cambridge, MA: Da Capo Press, 2008.

Marcus, Clare Cooper. *House as a Mirror of Self: Exploring the Deeper Meaning of Home.* Lake Worth, FL: Nicolas-Hays, 2006.

Pink, Daniel H. *A Whole New Mind: Why Right-Brainers Will Rule the Future.* New York: Penguin/Riverhead Books, 2005.

Shaw, Judith. "Why Is Creative Expression Important to the Human Soul?," Life on the Edge [blog], May 1, 2009, https://judithshaw.wordpress.com

index

photography credits

All photos copyright CICO Books and Ryland Peters and Small, unless otherwise stated.

Front cover: Sandra Lane; back cover (top): Rachel Whiting; back cover (bottom): Mark Scott; page 1: Debi Treloar; page 2: Catherine Gratwicke; page 3: Emma Mitchell; page 4: Rachel Whiting; page 5: Joanna Henderson; page 6: James Gardiner; page 9: Catherine Gratwicke; page 11: Catherine Gratwicke; page 13: Debi Treloar; page 14: Simon Brown; page 17: Polly Wreford; page 21: Rachel Whiting; page 23: Simon Brown; page 24: Mark Scott; page 27: Debi Treloar; page 29: Catherine Gratwicke; page 30: Simon Brown; page 32: Rachel Whiting; page 35: Rachel Whiting; page 36: Debi Treloar; page 38: Rachel Whiting; page 41: Polly Wreford; page 42: James Gardiner; page 45: Simon Brown; page 47: Simon Brown; page 48: Rachel Whiting; page 50: Mark Scott; page 52: Polly Wreford; page 53: Rachel Whiting; page 54: Mark Scott; page 56: Emma Mitchell; page 58: Joanna Henderson; page 61: Simon Brown; page 62: Beth Evans; page 64: Polly Wreford; page 67: Beth Evans; page 68: Debi Treloar; page 71: Rachel Whiting; page 72: Rachel Whiting; page 75: Debi Treloar; page 76: Debi Treloar; page 79: Mark Lohman; page 81: Rachel Whiting; page 82: Rachel Whiting; page 84: Rachel Whiting; page 85: Polly Wreford; page 87: Ian Wallace; page 88: Polly Wreford; page 91: Debi Treloar; page 93: Rachel Whiting; page 94: Rachel Whiting; page 97: Catherine Gratwicke; page 98: Mark Scott; page 101: Mark Scott; page 103: Polly Wreford; page 104: Polly Wreford; page 105: Jan Baldwin; page 107: Polly Wreford; page 108: Rachel Whiting; page 111: Rachel Whiting; page 112: Rachel Whiting; page 115: Rachel Whiting; page 116: Rachel Whiting; page 119: Catherine Gratwicke; page 120: Debi Treloar; page 122: James Gardiner; page 124: Rachel Whiting; page 126: Simon Brown; page 129: Catherine Gratwicke; page 130: Rachel Whiting; page 133: Debi Treloar; page 134: Dan Duchars; page 136: Polly Wreford; page 139: Polly Wreford; page 140: Polly Wreford; page 143: Emma Mitchell; page 145: Debi Treloar; page 146: Debi Treloar; page 148: Emma Mitchell; page 149: Polly Wreford; page 151: Helen Cathcart; page 152: Catherine Gratwicke; page 155: Simon Brown; page 156: Andrew Wood; page 159: Debi Treloar; page 160: Simon Brown; page 163: Simon Brown; page 164: Catherine Gratwicke; page 167: Paul Massey; page 169: Christopher Drake; page 170: Simon Brown.

acknowledgments

The number of people who've been part of this journey are too many to count, but I want to shout out a special thank you to the following humans—and several cats—who made this all possible:

Thank you to my husband Damian. You make every day feel like I'm living in a romantic comedy. You dance with me in the living room, cheer me on, and make sure I'm well-fed even when I work late, step up as an incredible co-host at every house party, and you're the world's best travel partner! It may be a cliché, but home truly is wherever you are.

Thank you to my parents. I was lucky enough to end up with four of you and double up on all the love, encouragement, and good old fashioned parental advice. Dad, you model what it looks like to stay true to one's values. Jack, you taught me to look my finances in the eye and be responsible for my choices and my money. Linda, you showed us all how to make a house a home no matter how many times we had to move as an Army family. And Mom, you taught me to think creatively and positively, and to make the best of everything. If I am decent human who wrote a decent book, I have you four to thank for it.

Thank you Carolyn, Kelly, Aimee, Natalie, Michelle, and Emily for encouraging me to embrace being a #girlboss, being there through the meltdowns, and understanding that sometimes whiskey is the answer.

Thank you Kristine, Cindy, and Anna at CICO Books for believing in the message of this book and helping to make it stronger than I ever could have done on my own.

Thank you to my seriously wonderful staff at Seriously Happy Homes. Every day you make the mission of this book a reality and help folks get happy at home.

And finally, a moment of gratitude to forty-two years of feline companions: Sweetheart, Tiffany, Rags, Honey, BeBop, Natasha, Lucy, and Murray. The world is a better place because it includes cats.